P9-BIB-988

IN TIMES OF CHALLENGE: CHICANOS AND CHICANAS IN AMERICAN SOCIETY

NATIONAL ASSOCIATION FOR CHICANO STUDIES

Editorial Committee
Juan R. García, Chair
Julia Curry Rodriguez
Clara Lomas

Mexican American Studies
Monograph Series No. 6
Mexican American Studies Program
University of Houston
Houston, Texas 77004

ISBN 0-939709-05-8

Library of Congress No. 88-060483

Cover designed by Hector Gonzalez

CONTENTS

INTRODUCTION

The articles and essays in this anthology were selected from papers presented at the 13th Annual Conference of the National Association for Chicano Studies, which convened in Sacramento, California, in March of 1985. Although the theme of the conference centered on Chicana/o political concerns in the 1980s and beyond, the papers included in this volume demonstrate that participants engaged a wide-ranging discussion of other topics and issues. Because of the diverse nature of the papers selected for inclusion in this volume, they have been grouped into three sections, each of which encompasses an overarching theme.

Politics in its various and sundry forms constitutes the theme of the articles written by Christine Sierra, Sylvia Lizarraga, and Richard Griswold del Castillo in Part I. In "Chicano Politics-After 1984", Professor Sierra provides an overview of politics in the Mexican American community during the 1980s. In the process she assesses recent gains in representation at the local, state and national level, and how Chicanas/os and other Hispanic groups have fared under the Reagan administration. The essay addresses a number of questions, such as: Has Chicano political power increased? Has an "Hispanic strategy" for organization benefitted Chicanas/os? And what forms will Chicano politics assume after 1984? She concludes her study by advancing some of her own ideas for a Chicano political agenda for the remainder of this decade.

While Sierra is interested in examining the plight of Chicanas/os within the political system of the United States, Sylvia Lizarraga is concerned with the application and formulation of theoretical precepts to analyze the experience of Chicanas. Her paper, "Toward a Theory of Women's Liberation," examines the complex interconnection of women's economic exploitation, and their patriarchal and racial oppression. Lizarraga explains the fundamental differences between the feminism of Third World women and that of middle class white women in the United States. A major difference she points to is that the struggle for emancipation by Third World women has been defined historically not only as one against patriarchal ideology, but also as a simultaneous struggle against economic exploitation and political oppression. She notes that even though the theoretical formulations posited by socialist feminists in the United States provide the foundations for the analysis of capitalist patriarchy, these have not yet provided for a complete analysis of the oppression of women of color in this country based upon class, race and sex. After discussing Zillah Eisentein's model, Lizarraga examines some of the causes and consequences of the internalization of racial discrimination by women. She concludes that women's complete liberation will not come about until all people committed to social change develop a political consiousness and take concrete action against the class exploitation, sexual oppression and racial discrimination which serve to subjugate women.

Richard Griswold del Castillo's essay, "the Chicano Movement and the Treaty of Guadalupe Hidalgo," provides an historical overview of how different groups within the Chicano community have interpreted and utilized the treaty to develop their plan of action and rationale for political action. For example Reies Lopez Tijerina was one of the first Chicano activists to provoke a reassessment of the treaty when he undertook his campaign to regain community land grants in New Mexico by arguing that legitimate treaty rights had been violated. In Denver, Chicano activists led by Rudolfo "Corky" Gonzales, joined forces with Tijerina in demanding that the land grants be returned to their rightful owners and that compensation be paid to those who had spent their hard-earned money in order to save their land. Professor del Castillo then discusses how the Brown Berets used the treaty to justify the take over of Catalina Island in 1972 and what they accomplished as a result of their 24 day occupation. Although this effort was overshadowed by the more dramatic events at Kit Carson National Forest and the shootout at Tierra Amarilla, del Castillo argues that the actions at Catalina Island demonstrated the degree to which some Chicanos were willing to challenge historical violations of the treaty.

Part II contains articles which explore the cultural aspects of the Chicana/o experience. In "Assimilation Revisited," Professor Renato Rosaldo discusses the question of assimilation and its costs to Chicanas/os. Through his analysis and critique of three major works on assimilation by Douglas Massey, Miriam Wells, and José Limon, he raises and responds to such questions as: Must Chicanas/os lose their cultural identity in order to improve their economic status? Does social mobility always lead to assimilation? Are social mobility and assimilation the same thing? Rosaldo argues that assimilation has been a process which has been poorly understood. He suggests that it might be better to conceive of it as a heterogenous contradictory phenomenon rather than as a linear trend.

As Chicano Studies gradually receives more attention in European universities, studies by European scholars have appeared which attempt to understand and explain the Chicano experience through its literary production. Lauro Flores' article, "En Torno a la 'Teoria de las Dos Cultures' y su Aplicacion a Literatura Chicana" is an examination of German Professor Dieter Herms' study of Chicano literature and his application of Lenin's theory of two cultures to interpret the Chicano experience. Flores points out that in spite of Herms' well-intentioned effort to analyze Chicano cultural production within an idelogical and socio-historical theoretical framework, the misapplication of Lenin's theory ultimately leads to the development of several misinterpretations of the very experience he is striving to understand. These misinterpretations, according to Flores, can be traced to theoretical, ideological, and expository problems present in Herms' approach. The result is that Herms' analysis is ahistorical, acritical and non-dialectical, and that it imparts a static representation of Chicano reality. Flores concludes that this reality is understood as a homogeneous phenomenon, without class distinctions or conflicting world views, which in the final analysis negates its complexity and specificity within a larger continental and hemispheric context.

Lawrence Benton's essay contains aspects of Rosaldo's and Flores' work on assimilation and literature in its interpretation of two Chicano novels. Benton focuses

2

on the themes of anticlericalism and assimilation in Jose Antonio Villareal's **Pocho,** and Tomas Rivera's **Y no se lo trago la tierra.** In **Pocho** the protagonist rejects the Catholicism of his parents because he considers it incompatible with the idea of individualism. In Rivera's work the hero rejects and curses God because of the All Mighty's apparent disregard and indifference to the poor. According to Professor Benton, Rivera's story explores the issues of class conflict and social justice. It is also an attack on religion as an instrument through which the exploitation of people is encouraged and justified. In **Pocho,** on the other hand, Villareal replaces the Catholic faith with an ideology that places emphasis on individualism and free choice as a means of resisting and overcoming exploitation. In both novels the respective authors have used the idea of anticlericalism to achieve diametrically opposed ends.

The study by Raymond Buriel and Desdemona Cardoza examines another aspect of Chicano/a culture by assessing the effect of Spanish-language background on the achievement levels of first, second and third generation Mexican-descent seniors. To ascertain if the effects of non-linguistic socio-economic background variables on achievement were the same for other students, the study utilized a sample of Anglo-American students. Another variable examined was the effect of mothers' aspirations on the achievement levels of students. The findings in "The Relationship of Spanish Language Background to Academic Achievement," indicate that the effects of Spanish on the achievement levels of Mexican descent students were minimal.

Celestino Fernandez's article "Resistance to Naturalization Among Mexican Immigrants: Causes and Consequences," discusses why Mexican immigrants choose to become naturalized. According to Professor Fernandez, the low naturalization rates among Mexican immigrants, which date back to the beginning of the 20th century, can be attributed to a variety of reasons and factors. After dilineating the reasons, he turns to a discussion of the data he gathered on naturalized Mexican immigrants and Mexicans who had not become citizens. He found that background characteristics, structural conditions, and cultural forces were all important variables which influenced the decision of Mexican immigrants to naturalize or not be naturalized. Fernandez concludes his study by proposing programs designed to assist immigrants, and encouraging that more studies on the subject be undertaken by researchers.

The articles in Part III explore historical issues and events. In "The Los Angeles Police Department and Mexican Workers," Professor Edward Escobar describes the series of events that led to and culminated in the so-called Christmas Riot of 1913 in Los Angeles. The "riot" broke out when members of the Los Angeles Police Department disrupted a rally held by Mexicans to protest low wages and poor working conditions. As a result one man was killed and over seventy protesters, most of whom were of Mexican descent, were arrested. Escobar then details the court proceedings which followed. Ten of the defendants were found guilty despite evidence the police had wrongfully violated the rights of the protesters and had themselves been responsible for much of the violence which had erupted during the meeting. Professor Escobar argues that the incident was symptomatic of the relationship between Mexicans in Los Angeles and the L.A.P.D. He also believes that the police force was the instrument of Southern California business interests, and that its role was to suppress labor union activity and other forms of social protest among Mexicans.

Professor Ruben Martinez's study is a follow-up to the work done on the social, economic and political conditions of the **Taosenos** of northern New Mexico by George I. Sanchez in the 1930s. In "The Rediscovery of the Forgotten People," Martinez assesses the changes experienced by these people during the five decades which followed by focusing on demographic and labor market forces in the region. He concludes that promises of economic development and improvement have gone largely unfulfilled, and that the **Taosenos** have enjoyed few if any benefits. The lack of economic opportunity in the region has forced many to seek employment elsewhere, which has had an adverse impact on the native population. Those who have remained have found work in a system characterized by a racial division of labor.

In "La Vision de la Frontera a Traves del Cine Mexicano," Lic. Norma Iglesias presents an analysis of how the northern border region has been depicted in Mexican commercial films. Iglesias states that movies have played an important role in mystifying and stereotyping the border. Her study encompasses the years between 1938 and 1969. The films produced during these years are divided into three periods to faciliate discussion and analysis. The author is critical of the false and misleading images created by the majority of these films, and discusses their harmful and negative impact. She concludes by calling for a more realistic and balanced depiction of the border in Mexican films.

The publications and annual conferences sponsored by NACS are intended to provide a forum for the exchange of ideas, viewpoints and research in order to promote a greater understanding of the Chicana/o experience. The papers selected for publication in this anthology explore different facets of that experience. In the process, they have raised a number of questions about the present status of Chicanas/os in American society during the so-called "Decade of the Hispanic." Those questions, which concern educational achievement, treaty rights, immigration, assimilation, police-community relations, political participation, and issues related to gender, provide a framework in which we can begin to address the issues and challenges which lie before us collectively and as individuals. It is to that ideal that this collection of essays and articles is dedicated.

The Editorial Committee wishes to thank the authors whose contributions made this anthology possible. Special acknowledgment goes to Editorial Committee members Clara Lomas and Julia Curry Rodriguez, whose skill, hard work and dedication made this project a rewarding and pleasant experience. The Committee also wishes to acknowledge the assistance of Professor Tatcho Mindiola, Jr. and the Mexican American Studies Program at the University of Houston, for sponsoring the publication of this volume.

Juan R. García, Chair

Julia Curry Rodriguez

Clara Lomas

Editorial Committee
National Association for Chicano Studies

Part I

POLITICS

CHICANO POLITICS—AFTER 1984

Christine Marie Sierra

ABSTRACT

This article provides an overview of politics in the Mexican American community during the decade of the 1980s. Analysis focuses on recent gains in political representation, the impact of Reagan Administration policies on the Chicano community, and the Latino vote for President in 1984. The conclusion identifies several concerns that will shape the Chicano political agenda for the rest of the decade.

In order to discuss Chicano politics after 1984, Chicano politics before and during 1984 must be assessed. At the outset of this decade, an optimistic message appeared in popular magazines and even on billboards of corporate America. The message proclaimed the 1980s to be the "Decade of the Hispanic." While there were die-hard skeptics in the Chicano community who doubted the validity of such a proclamation, there were many others who were attracted to it.

Those who optimistically (or perhaps opportunistically) saw the 1980s turning into an "Hispanic decade" pointed to Latinos' increasing numbers, both absolute and relative, in the U.S. population as a source of political strength. The assumption was that numbers translate into votes, votes translate into power, and power translates into a better quality of life in American society.

Accordingly, "Hispanisization" of the Mexican, Puerto Rican, Cuban, and other Spanish-origin populations gained popularity in the 1980s. This "Hispanisization" produced even greater numbers and more visibility for each individual group as part of a new whole. In concert with other Spanish-origin groups, Chicano(a)s were expected to increase their political strength in American society and, consequently, derive more benefits from the system.

What did Chicano(a)s gain from politics before and during 1984? Has Chicano political power increased? Has an "Hispanic strategy" for organization worked to benefit them as a group? What forms will Chicano politics take—after 1984?

This essay addresses these questions by outlining the parameters of Chicano political development in the 1980s. Based on these observations, some considerations for a Chicano political agenda in the last half of this decade will be advanced.

7

RECENT GAINS IN CHICANO POLITICAL REPRESENTATION

The 1980s have produced some measurable gains in Chicano political strength. Gains in political representation have resulted from increasing numbers *and* pressure group politics. For example, Chicanos and other Latinos monitored the 1980 census process in order to obtain a more accurate count of the burgeoning Latino population.[1] These efforts sought to insure that Latino interests would be enhanced when reapportionment of state and congressional districts, based on the 1980 Census, took place. In addition, Chicano groups fought alongside other civil rights organizations for the extension of the Voting Rights Act in 1982.[2] These accomplishments and previous reapportionment activities in the 1970s bolstered Chicano efforts in the 1980s to open the electoral process even further to Chicano participation.[3]

Groups such as the Southwest Voter Registration Education Project (SVREP) and the Mexican American Legal Defense and Educational Fund (MALDEF) have used litigation very successfully to win redistricting fights in a number of states, including Texas, New Mexico, California, and Illinois.[4] Successful reapportionment battles have also been waged at the city level.

In Chicago, four new Hispanic wards were created as a result of a lawsuit filed by MALDEF and the Puerto Rican Legal Defense and Educational Fund in 1982.[5] Significantly, redistricting of Chicago's ward system allowed Mayor Harold Washington to gain control of the Chicago city council in the 1986 aldermanic elections.[6]

Litigation aimed at replacing at-large election systems with single-member district elections has also furthered Chicano interests. As MALDEF Association Counsel José Garza explains, at-large elections dilute the impact of the Hispanic vote, whereas "single-member district elections are simply more representative."[7] They increase the chances of Latino(a)s winning elective office. In summary, effective interest group politics, combined with significant increases in the Latino population during the 1970s, advanced Chicano political representation in the first part of the decade.

Representation at the National Level

Electoral success can be demonstrated at the national level by looking at Chicano and other Latino representation in Congress. At the outset of the 1980s, Latinos in Congress numbered five voting members and one non-voting delegate. All were in the House of Representatives. Chicano legislators, all of whom were elected in the 1960s, included Edward Roybal (D-CA), Manuel Lujan (R-NM), Henry B. González (D-TX), and E. Kika de la Garza (D-TX). They were joined by Puerto Rican Congressman Robert García (D-NY) who was elected in 1978. The non-voting delegate was Baltasar Corrada from Puerto Rico.[8]

Elections in 1982 ushered in four new Chicanos into the House of Representatives. They were Esteban Torres and Matthew Martínez from California, Bill Richardson from New Mexico, and Solomon Ortiz from Texas. All Democrats, they were elected from new districts created through reapportionment.[9] In 1984 another Chicano representative, Albert Bustamante, a Democrat from South Texas, joined the Hispanic delegation. Thus, in just four years, Latino representation in Congress increased by five, doubling the number of Hispanic voting members in Congress.

The Hispanic delegation in Congress is still few in number. They constitute only a tiny fraction of the total number (435) in the House of Representatives. Furthermore, no Latino(a) sits in the United States Senate. Nevertheless, the recent increase in their numbers has given them more visibility as they seek to promote Latino interests through their own legislative group, the Congressional Hispanic Caucus.

The Caucus emerged in December of 1976, largely at the urging of Congressman Edward Roybal. Initially Chicano and Puerto Rican legislators conferred informally among themselves on legislative priorities. No office or staff existed for the Caucus until 1978. In the 1980s the Caucus began to institutionalize itself more formally "to develop a united congressional effort on behalf of Hispanic Americans."[10] Caucus members began meeting on a regular basis, and the group increased its legislative activities.

In recent years the Caucus has broadened the definition of Hispanic to include among its members Representative Tony Coelho (D-CA), of Portuguese descent, and Democrat Ron de Lugo and Republican Ben Blaz, non-voting delegates from the Virgin Islands and Guam, respectively. While their addition has increased the Hispanic Caucus membership to 14, it remains to be seen if the Caucus' political clout increases accordingly.

Because it is bipartisan and its members are increasing in their diversity, some scholars and lobbyists question the Caucus' ability to act as a cohesive legislative force within Congress.[11] The evidence indicates that when the members manage to speak in a united voice they can indeed be forceful advocates for Hispanic concerns. Such occurred when the Caucus formed a fairly cohesive lobby against the Simpson-Mazzoli immigration bill in 1984. Combined with the Black Congressional Caucus, they constituted serious opposition to the passage of restrictive immigration legislation in the 98th Congress.

Expansion of the Caucus' size in Congress is important. The Caucus can acquire more visibility and stature within the institution. However, an increase in sheer numbers may have its political tradeoffs. If Caucus members reflect great diversity in ideological perspective, Caucus efforts to forge a consensus on issues will be hindered. Consequently, its legislative agenda will most likely narrow in scope.

The legislative agenda will include only those issues on which all or most members can agree. Issues that revolve around language and cultural rights (bilingualism), constitutional guarantees (voting rights), and socioeconomic advancement could constitute consensus issues. Across Latino groups, support for these types of issues appears to be fairly strong. Recent surveys of Latino communities in the Southwest and Midwest indicate clear majorities favor bilingual education and protection of the Voting Rights Act.[12] In sum, Caucus activity may concentrate only on those issues which enjoy relatively widespread support within the Latino community.

At the same time, the Caucus' potential to provide leadership on controversial issues of public policy may diminish. Ironically, issues that are controversial within and across Latino groups demand *more* not less attention to resolve them. Debate, clarification, and resolution of such issues would in the long run promote a more cohesive Latino power bloc.

Representation at the State and Local Levels

Overall, the number of Latinos in elective office doubled from 1973 to 1984. In addition to the U.S. Representatives, Latino state and local officials in 1984 ranged from one governor to 1,173 school board members for a total of 3,128 public officeholders.[13] These gains in representation, however, did not impact equally at the state and local levels.

At the state level, observes political scientist John García Chicanos mostly "held on to the seats they gained in state legislatures in the mid-1970s." García notes that the sun-belt migration of Anglos to the Southwest was one factor that held Chicano representation at the state level in check. He explains, "Despite significant growth within the Chicano community, relative gains were offset by non-Chicano in-migrants coming from the Midwest and other regions."[14]

Noticeable increases in Chicano representation occurred at the local level. Beyond the Chicano "celebrity" mayors, Henry Cisneros of San Antonio and Federico Peña of Denver, Chicano(a)s increased their numbers in municipal, county, and school board positions across the country.[15]

Greater electoral success rates at the local level can be partially attributed to the following factors. First, Chicano political experience emanates from community based politics. Local political arenas have been easier to penetrate and influence than state and national political forums. Chicano political activism, whether expressed through elections, organizations, or protests, has largely been aimed at local level institutions and policies.

Second, Chicano(a)s may be more interested in local concerns than national or international issues.[16] Willie Velasquez, Executive Director of the Southwest Voter Registration Education Project, has made such an observation based on his experience in conducting voter registration drives in numerous Chicano communities throughout the country.[17] Political scientists have long found that a significant percentage of Americans feel that "politics and government are too complicated." Certainly, local issues have an immediacy to them that can make the complicated (or seemingly irrelevant) world of politics very tangible in people's everyday lives.[18]

Recognizing the issue saliency of local concerns, Chicano groups have launched voter registration and education drives that have emphasized local issues and electoral campaigns. Indeed, Alinsky-style organizations, such as Communities Organized for Public Service (COPS) in San Antonio and the El Paso Interreligious Sponsoring Organization (EPISO) in El Paso, Texas, have focussed very successfully on *neighborhood* issues to engage community residents in political action.

Finally, the size of a political unit and the percentage of Chicanos in it partially explain Chicano electoral success. John García finds that when Chicanos comprise a small percentage of a community (less than 10 percent) or are the majority group within it (65 percent and more), their chances of winning elective office increase. He suggests one interpretation of this pattern. Chicano(a)s tend to win elective office when: (1) their election represents a "non-threatening token" acquisition of power or simply individual mobility, or (2) Chicanos achieve "numerical dominance in the community."[19]

Some Lingering Concerns

While Chicano political representation has increased since the 1960s and 1970s, it is also true that Chicanos remain severely underrepresented at all levels of government. Most glaring is the underrepresentation of Latina women in elective office. No Latina sits in Congress. And only seven Latinas were to be found in state legislatures throughout the whole country prior to the 1984 elections (in Arizona, California, Colorado, Florida, New Mexico, New York, and Texas).[20] Only 12% of all elected positions held by Latinos throughout the country are held by women. This figure approximates the level of political underrepresentation for women in the society in general.[21]

Certainly class, racial, and gender biases inherent in the American political system underlie the political underrepresentation of Chicano(a)s. Structural obstacles to minority group participation in elections persist. Whites continue to favor white candidates over minority candidates. And, like other groups who have been historically "disconnected" from mainstream American politics, Chicano(a)s reflect lower rates of voter registration and turnout than the general population.[22]

Some special demographic characteristics of the Mexican origin community partially account for the lower levels of electoral participation. In comparison to other groups, the Mexican origin population has lower levels of education, a high percentage of youths under voting age, and a significant percentage of legal resident aliens (non-citizens) with low naturalization rates.[23] Such factors prevent the group's numbers from translating directly into votes and political offices.

Chicanas, of course, face special obstacles to penetrating public spheres of power dominated by men. As with other women, childrearing responsibilities and fewer economic resources tend to prevent them from running for office.[24] Moreover, negative attitudes towards women in politics are still very much alive, if not always publicly acknowledged. Gloria Molina pointed to male resistance to her campaign as one serious obstacle she had to overcome in becoming the first Chicana ever to sit in the California State Assembly.[25]

In summary, despite the obstacles, political advances have been made. However, Chicano(a)s are entitled to vastly more offices and elective positions in terms of their relative numbers (or percent) in the population. Stated another way, "formal representation" has increased, but *parity* or equity for Chicano(a)s is still sorely lacking.

Furthermore, formal representation, while important, does not necessarily reveal the extent to which minority groups are *effectively* or fairly represented by "their own kind" and others in office. Scholarship in urban and race politics underscores how various types of representation can enhance or hinder the promotion of minority group interests.[26]

For example, the election of minority group representatives to a city council may be symbolically important but result in few tangible group benefits. A recent study of Black and Hispanic politics in northern California argues that the *incorporation* of minority groups into liberal coalitions that dominate decision-making in city hall is essential for the furtherance of minority group interests in local-level politics.[27]

In the end, building Chicano political power involves more than a "numbers game." It also involves the creation of mechanisms of accountability—to hold political elites, be they Chicano or non-Chicano—accountable to the wishes and interests of their Chicano constituencies. Organization to force the collective empowerment of Mexican origin communities across the country remains of vital importance.

Policies responsive to the needs of Chicano communities must result from the placement of individuals in public office. Grassroots pressure must work to secure elite responsiveness in policymaking. Accordingly, the establishment of mechanisms to impart political knowledge and skills at the grassroots level cannot be overlooked. Strengthening individuals' ability to make independent assessments of their political world should result from such efforts. In addition, expanding opportunities for

11

political expression, both within and outside electoral politics, can only enhance Chicano political power at all levels.

CHICANOS AND THE REAGAN ADMINISTRATION

Another question to be raised when evaluating Chicano political development in the 1980s is how has this community fared in this era of national conservatism? Chicano communities before, during, and after 1984 have had to contend with the insidious policies and cold war ideology of the Reagan Administration.

The Impact of Reagan Policies

Census data and studies such as those produced by the Urban Institute in Washington, D.C. and the Southwest Voter Registration and Education Project (SVREP) document what is transpiring in Mexican and Latino communities across the country. "Trickle down" economics is not working for the vast majority of this population. In particular, rising levels of poverty and unemployment plus cutbacks in social programs have had devastating effects on working class and poor families.

Poverty in the Latino population has been increasing for some time. However, since 1980 poverty among Latino(a)s has increased at a faster rate. Especially troubling is the sharp rise in poverty among Latino children. In 1980, 35% of all Latino children under six lived in poverty. By 1983, 42% of Latino children under six were poor. The Southwest Voter Registration Education Project emphasizes that this increase "represents the most rapid increase in poverty for any racial, ethnic, or age group in America over this period." High levels of unemployment and Reagan budget cuts enacted since 1981 account for much of the rise in poverty.[28]

Reagan's economic policies are not benefitting the average Latino working family. In 1972 the median Hispanic family income was 71% of the median Anglo family income. In 1983, that percentage fell to 66% of Anglo family income.[29] Indeed, during Reagan's first term in office, the income gap between the wealthiest 40% of the U.S. population and the poorest 40% was at its widest point since 1947. A majority of Latinos were in the poorest 40% bracket (nearly 60% of all Latino families have incomes of less than $20,000 a year).[30]

Both the Urban Institute and the Congressional Budget Office (CBO) assessed the overall impact of Reagan's first-term budget cuts and tax policies. They produced similar results. Low and moderate income families disproportionately suffered the burdens of budget cuts and income loss.[31] Some figures drive the point home:

> Nearly half of the budget cuts fell on households with incomes below $10,000 a year, and 70 percent of the cuts fell on households below $20,000 a year. . . .
> Only one percent of the cuts were borne by households over $80,000 a year.[32]

As their poverty and unemployment increases, family incomes fall, and social programs of particular importance to the group are whittled away, Chicano(a)s appear to be on the losing end of the so-called economic recovery of the 1980s.

Chicano Policy Preferences in the Reagan Era

Studies of Chicano public opinion show that their policy preferences, as a group, conflict with the policies of the Reagan Administration. According to recent survey data, unemployment and inflation have been uppermost among Chicano concerns at the national level. Chicanos generally favor increased spending on social programs and bilingual education. They supported extension of the Voting Rights Act in 1982. They also favored in greater proportion than that of the general population passage of the Equal Rights Amendment.[33]

On foreign policy and defense issues, Chicano(a)s favor a *decrease* in spending for defense, space programs, and foreign aid.[34] Moreover, surveys of Chicano voters in Texas and the Midwest in 1984 show strong opposition to U.S. military aid to the government of El Salvador and to the Contras in Nicaragua.[35]

All of these positions run counter to the policies and actions of the Reagan Administration. Only on the question of legalized abortion have there been some "Reaganesque" opinions among Chicanos. Forty-seven percent support legalized abortion "under certain circumstances" and 34% oppose abortion under any circumstances.[36]

Evidence points out that Chicanos, as a group, are statistically worse off under Reaganomics. Their policy preferences indicate that they are opposed to Reagan policies. An important question to assess, then, is to what extent did Chicanos support Ronald Reagan's reelection in 1984?

The Chicano Vote for President in 1984

Table 1 presents the results of national exit polls conducted by the three major networks. Although the results vary,[37] they all show that a majority of Latinos did not support Ronald Reagan for President. At the same time, Latinos voted to a greater extent for Reagan than did Blacks.

Table 1
National Exit Poll Results of Vote for President, 1984

	NBC NEWS		CBS NEWS/NYT		ABC/WP	
	R*	M	R	M	R	M
Whites	66%	34%	66%	34%	63%	36%
Latinos	32%	68%	33%	65%	43%	56%
Blacks	9%	91%	9%	90%	11%	89%

*Note: R = President Ronald Reagan
      M = Democratic Party candidate Walter Mondale

Sources: Robert R. Brischetto, "Latinos in the 1984 Election Exit Polls: Some Findings and Some Methodological Lessons," paper presented at Conference, "Ignored Voices: Public Opinion Polls and the Latino Community," sponsored by The Center for Mexican American Studies, The University of Texas at Austin, October 18, 1985 (for NBC and ABC/Washington Post figures); and The New York Times/CBS News Poll, "Portrait of the Electorate," *The New York Times*, Thursday, November 8, 1984, p. 11.

Additional data suggest important differences among Latino groups. The Southwest Voter Registration Education Project provides the following data based on statewide and citywide exit polls and voting in selected Hispanic precincts across the country.[38]

The clearest division in the Hispanic vote appears to be between Cubans and the other major subgroups, Puerto Ricans and Chicanos. Cubans in Miami indicated they supported Reagan by a 9-to-1-ratio. Two statewide polls in Florida confirmed strong support among Cuban voters for Reagan. In Union City, New Jersey, Cuban support for Reagan ran equally strong (87%). Reagan also garnered a majority of the Cuban vote in New York City.[39]

Only data from the Midwest indicate a possible deviation from strong Cuban support for Reagan. However, because of small sample sizes, Cuban voters were combined with those of South and Central American ancestry. Consequently, the results may be misleading. The Midwest survey indicated a majority of this combined category of Latino voters supported Mondale, 56.7% to 43.3%.[40]

Solid Cuban support for Reagan is at least partially based upon support for Reagan's stand on Central America. According to pollster John Lasseville of the Spanish International Network (SIN), his polls show that Cubans have been most concerned with "the situation in Central America."[41] Consequently, Reagan's cold war stand on "communist aggression" in Central American has endeared him to Cubanos.

In contrast, Chicanos and Puerto Ricans supported Walter Mondale in the 1984 presidential election. Texas Chicanos voted for Mondale 75% to 24%. Only 28% of the Chicano voters in East Los Angeles voted for Ronald Reagan. New York City Puerto Ricans show a strikingly similar pattern; 27% voted for Reagan.[42]

Texas data from the Southwest Voter Registration Education Project permit further analysis of the Chicano vote in 1984.[43] Republicans made some inroads into the traditionally Democratic Chicano vote, but only in a limited way. First, there were no gender differences among Chicanos on who they preferred for President. Women and men disliked Ronald Reagan equally! In contrast, gender gaps appear in the general population and among Puerto Ricans. In both cases, women showed more disapproval (or less support) for Reagan than their male counterparts.[44]

Younger Chicano voters favored Ronald Reagan more than older voters; but overall, a majority of young Chicanos favored Mondale. Where Republicans seemed to have made inroads to the Mexican vote was in certain income brackets. Republicans drew support from those at the top ranks of the income ladder—from those whose annual incomes were $50,000 and over. This is, of course, a very tiny sector—three percent—of the total Mexican origin population.[45]

In the end, those Chicanos who voted for Reagan in 1984 probably did so for some of the same reasons that the general population as a whole voted for Reagan. They perhaps perceived the state of the economy as improving and affecting them in a positive way. Maybe they saw inflation going down and jumped on the Ronald Reagan bandwagon. There could have been some issue voting on abortion.

Despite some Chicanos voting for Reagan in '84, overall the vast majority voted against him. As the authors of the series on the Chicano electorate conclude, Chicanos in the 1980s constitute a cohesive electorate, one that reflects a collective experience in American politics and society. And one that will not be easily persuaded by conservative Republican appeals.[46]

THE HISPANIC AGENDA FOR THE REST OF THE DECADE

What does the rest of the decade hold for the development of Chicano political power? An "Hispanic agenda" now calls for moving beyond "recognition politics''[47] to an institutionalization of power. The institutionalization of power is particularly critical during the second-term presidency of Ronald Reagan. Several concerns can be identified for the years ahead.

(1) The first observation: Strengthened by the current political climate, the rise of the New Right and the institutionalization of its own power carry implications for minority group politics for the remainder of this decade and beyond. The New Right's well-organized and well-financed pressure group politics constitute a countervailing power to Black and Latino forces.

For example, Black and Latino groups launched massive voter registration drives for the '84 election. But so did conservative forces of the Right—and very successfully, too. The Republican Party itself financed a highly centralized voter registration campaign in twenty-eight states. According to the *Washington Post*, the ''high-tech'' GOP campaign, which cost $10 million, ''was supplemented by major drives to enroll white conservative fundamentalist Christians.''[48]

The 1984 Texas race for the U.S. Senate also serves as an illustration of the forces of the Right. Racial tensions were heightened in the Democratic party primary run-off when one candidate resorted to racist scare tactics in promoting his own election and the defeat of his two moderate/liberal opponents.

U.S. Representative Kent Hance (D-TX) ran television commercials proclaiming that Texan interests were threatened by the invasion of ''illegal aliens.'' Hance used to his advantage the issue of ''amnesty'' for undocumented workers, pending in immigration legislation before Congress. He charged that he would oppose an ''amnesty'' program in Congress whereas his opponents would not.

Hance's commercials infuriated Chicano groups in Texas who tried to counteract his tactics. The National Council of La Raza reminded Hance of his publicly stated concern about the discriminatory impact of employer sanctions against Hispanics. The Council wrote to the Congressman:

> There are those in this country and in Texas who fail to distinguish the difference between undocumented workers and Hispanic Americans. Commercials which incite fear of, and resentment against, undocumented immigrants, therefore, risk creating the very kind of discrimination you claim to be concerned about.[49]

Hance lost the Democratic party nomination to Lloyd Doggett, who was heavily favored by Chicano voters, but he gained great political mileage for himself. He subsequently switched his affiliation to the Republican Party. In the end, Republican Phil Gramm won easily over Doggett in the general election. Voting in Texas was racially polarized, and the Republicans benefited from this polarization. It is quite likely that as Chicanos become more organized, they will encounter greater organized opposition from the Right, at least for the remainder of this decade.

(2) A second observation: The role of electoral politics in the development of an Hispanic political bloc as well as alliances based on race, class, and gender will be put to a test. Recent scholarship on Black politics suggests that we are in an era of a revitalized political strategy. That is, Black people are turning again to electoral politics, but in a new way:

> Electoral activism is not perceived as an end in itself, but as a tool to mobilize not only blacks in American cities, but also poor and working-class people of all races and nationalities. This orientation utilizes electoral activism as a dialectical and educational process.[50]

Thus, electoral politics provide the arena for the mobilization of subordinate groups to challenge dominant ideologies and dominant class interests in American politics. Jesse Jackson's Rainbow Coalition serves as an example of the "new Black politics."

Black scholar Manning Marable describes Reverend Jackson's 1984 presidential bid as a campaign that "became a broadly democratic social protest movement, initiated and led by black people, which *assumed an electoral form.*"[51] Jackson challenged the Democratic party to respond to the needs and interests of the underclass, the disenfranchised, the underrepresented in American society. His criticism of Reagan administration policies at times entailed a critique of corporate capitalism and the racist underpinnings of American foreign policy.

Although limited in its overall impact on traditional party politics, Jackson's campaign was significant. The Rainbow Coalition's mobilization strategy met with dramatic success in the Black community. Black voter participation rates soared. In the Southern primaries, Black voter turnout was proportionately higher than white voter turnout. A new electorate also participated. Roughly one-fifth of those who voted for Jackson were first-time voters.[52]

Jackson and his supporters have now turned to strengthening the organizational base of the Rainbow Coalition. Although never a Black-only movement, the Coalition seeks to increase its resources and multicultural membership in preparation for the 1988 presidential contest.[53]

Jackson and his rainbow have struck responsive chords among certain sectors of the Latino population. Some Chicano and Puerto Rican movement activists are "reentering" electoral politics and organizing for the Rainbow Coalition. In addition, rainbow-type coalition politics are developing in local areas as well. The election of Harold Washington as mayor of the windy city of Chicago is perhaps the best example.

Together Blacks and Latinos comprise a majority of Chicago's population. Blacks constitute over 40% and Latinos approximately 14–17% of the city's population.[54] A long-established political machine had kept these groups marginalized in city politics despite their numbers.

In April, 1983, Harold Washington made history when he became Chicago's first Black mayor. His election was the culmination of a grassroots movement that sought to wrest power from the Democratic party machine that had controlled city government for decades. The reform movement had its base in the Black community, but it also drew support from Latinos and the white liberal-left.

In the Democratic mayoral primary of February 1983, Washington defeated his white opponents as the result of strong Black support and a divided white vote. Blacks overwhelmingly supported Washington with 80% of their total vote. An estimated 89% of the white vote split almost evenly between the incumbent Mayor Jane Byrne and Richard M. Daley, son of Chicago's former machine boss. Washington received less than 8% of the total white vote. Latinos split their votes among the three candidates. Votes from Latino wards indicated 45% support for Byrne, 30% for Daley, and 25% for Washington.[55] Although Latinos did not favor Washington in the primary, they voted for him to a greater extent than whites.

Strong Latino support for Washington was evident by the general election. Unlike white Democrats who largely defected to the Republican candidate, Latinos increased their support for Washington. Additionally, more turned out to vote in the general election than in the primary. The rate of increase in Latino turnout ranged from 126% to over 400% in some wards.[56]

Overall, Latino wards gave Washington 74% of their total vote. Washington also captured 98% of the vote in Black wards and 12% of the vote in white wards. Consequently, a Black/Brown alliance, with help from the white liberal-left, gave Washington a victory with 50.06% of the total vote compared to Republican Bernard Epton's 46.4%.[57]

Latino organization and electoral support was critical to the Washington movement's success. As part of Washington's campaign staff, Latino(a) organizers mobilized support in their communities for Washington.[58] Significantly, the Washington campaign created a Black and Latino coalition that had not existed before. The reform movement also brought the various sectors of the Latino community together in an unprecedented fashion. Chicanos and Puerto Ricans, along with some Cuban activists, worked together in an unprecedented fashion. Chicanos and Puerto Ricans, along with some Cuban activists, worked together as never before.[59] All three Latino groups awarded Washington a majority of their votes in the general election.[60]

As one Latina activist cautiously observed, the Latino coalition "remains rather fragile" but continues to develop.[61] The same has been said for Black and Latino alliances under Washington's administration. Despite the developmental nature of these coalitions, Chicago's rainbow movement will not be easily turned back.

It is perhaps fantasy, at this point, to see a rainbow coalition taking hold across the country. But this type of coalition-building is certain to be on the Chicano political agenda for the rest of this decade.

(3) The third observation: The process of institutionalizing group power can become very problematic for Chicanos. It could result in the empowerment of only specialized sectors, specialized interests of the Chicano population. Class divisions are already emerging that result in a distancing of Chicano elites from the mass base. Co-optation and brokerage politics may in fact limit empowerment of the community significantly in the years ahead. Chicano(a)s must strengthen their ability to hold accountable those who speak on their behalf.

Grassroots community organizations are important in this regard. The leaders and activists involved in issues at the local, community level serve as a critical link between government officialdom and community interests. Notably the Alinsky organizations that have developed in Southwestern cities and in Chicago serve this purpose. Examples are the United Neighborhoods Organization (UNO) in Los Angeles, Valley Inter-Faith in the Texas Rio Grande Valley, and Chicago's Northwest Community Organization.

These organizations use pressure group tactics to make sure that politicians are held accountable and responsive to community demands. Moreover, they have cultivated a new grassroots political leadership composed largely of women. The Alinsky groups organize through the Catholic Church as they seek to recruit the "natural leaders" in local parishes.[62] This strategy has attracted Chicanas, many previously uninvolved in politics, to their fold. Indeed, Latinas now predominate in the leadership and membership of these organizations.

4) A fourth observation: A second Ronald Reagan term is producing a number of policies that are adversely affecting Chicanos and to which Chicano groups are trying to respond. The issues include the crisis in Central America, immigration reform, cutbacks in domestic social programs, and increased defense spending.

Numerous challenges lie ahead for the development of consensus within Chicano communities on these issues. Efforts must be made to educate the public on how these issues are *interrelated*. The adverse consequences of Reagan policies, national and international in scope, must be brought to bear on Chicano concerns at the local—and personal—level. Common interests within the Mexican origin community, regardless of one's legal status, must be clarified. Understanding of the diverse histories of other Latino groups, both within and outside this nation's borders, should be encouraged.

By virtue of their visibility, national Latino organizations and the Congressional Hispanic Caucus can play leading roles in meeting these challenges. Chicano intellectuals can also play a critical role by disseminating their research and analyses into public and policymaking arenas.

Above all, Chicano(a)s must begin to redefine the public discourse on "special interests." Chicano(a)s must insist that the promotion of their group interests promotes the national interest as well.

SUMMARY AND CONCLUSIONS

Let us now readdress some of the major points outlined in this essay. First, there is the argument that numbers (absolute and relative) translate into political strength in American politics. To a degree this is true. Political representation has increased, structural reforms of the electoral system have been won, and a national presence for Chicanos has been established. But to what degree have such visible forms of power translated into the actual empowerment of the Mexican origin community?

Institutional responsiveness to Chicano demands, policy agendas that speak to Chicano needs and interests, and elite accountability to community-based interests are questions still to be assessed.

A second point raised in this essay was the widespread belief that an "Hispanic strategy" would produce increased levels of political power and national recognition for Latinos in the decade of the 1980s. To be sure, there are identifiable Latino communities with shared experiences and overlapping interests. "Hispanisizing" this population has brought more national recognition to all subgroups, perhaps more than they would receive individually.

But Hispanisization has also resulted in a rather contrived political agenda for these groups. Hispanisization, largely a product of government pronouncements in the 1970s and 1980s, has clouded the divisions and differences across and within Latino groups. Until these divisions are addressed, and lines of cooperation *and* separatism defined, the so-called Hispanic coalition remains fragile.

Distinct historical experiences, class divisions, and ideological differences must be acknowledged and debated. A common identity born of shared experiences, shared inequities, shared oppression, must serve as the basis of mobilization across Latino groups—to produce a new and authentic collective identity.

In conclusion, while *mechanisms* or *forms* for gaining political power may be found throughout the American political system, societal resources, wealth, and power are *maldistributed* across American society. There is renewed interest among Blacks and Latinos to use electoral politics as a strategy for group mobilization and group empowerment. Among the progressive sectors of these minority communities, the fundamental goal is a redistribution of wealth and power across American society, and not simply political representation. Such is the articulated goal among community activists in Chicago who participated in Harold Washington's election. They saw Washington's campaign and election as components of a larger social movement—a movement pledged to redistribute power and wealth and to empower the oppressed.

18

At least for now, such goals remain fantasies. But some fantasies are worth fighting for—after 1984.

NOTES

1. Latino elected officials and organizations offered testimony on the 1980 Census in hearings before the House Subcommittee on Census and Population held in New York, New Jersey, California, and Texas. For Mexican American testimony, see U.S., Congress, House, Committee on Post Office and Civil Service, *Oversight Hearings on the 1980 Census—Parts VI, VII, VIII,* Hearings before the Subcommittee on Census and Population, 96th Congress, 1st session, May, 1979.
2. U.S., Congress, House, Committee on the Judiciary, *Extension of the Voting Rights Act, Parts 2 and 3,* Hearings before the Subcommittee on Civil and Constitutional Rights, 97th Congress, 1st session, June and July, 1981.
3. For a review of Chicano reapportionment activities spanning three decades, see Richard Santillán, "The Latino Community in State and Congressional Redistricting: 1961–1985," *Journal of Hispanic Politics* 1 (1985): 52–66.
4. *Ibid,* pp. 61–64.
5. Mexican American Legal Defense and Educational Fund, Inc., *MALDEF Newsletter,* Spring/Summer, 1983, p. 7, and January, 1986, p. 1.
6. Luis Burguillo, Legislative Representative, City of Chicago, Office of the Mayor, Washington, D.C., telephone conversation, May 12, 1986; Kevin Klose, "Vast Patronage Powers at Stake in Chicago Vote," *The Washington Post,* Saturday, March 15, 1986, p. A-3, and Klose, "Runoff Gives Mayor Effective Control of Chicago Council," *The Washington Post,* Thursday, May 1, 1986, p. A-3.
7. José Garza, MALDEF Associate Counsel in San Antonio, Texas, quoted in Mexican American Legal Defense and Educational Fund, Inc., *MALDEF Newsletter,* January, 1985, p. 7. Also see Santillán, "The Latino Community," p. 53.
8. Delegates in Congress are not allowed to vote on the House floor. However, they do vote in committees.
9. John A. García, "Chicano Political Development: Examining Participation in the Decade of Hispanics," National Chicano Council on Higher Education, *La Red/The Net,* No. 72, September, 1983, p. 9.
10. Congressional Hispanic Caucus, "The Congressional Hispanic Caucus," information sheet, 1985; interviews with the Caucus' legislative staff, Washington, D.C., December 1985.
11. Kevin Kelley, "Hispanic Caucus—Diverse Latino America Struggles to Find Single Political Voice," Pacific News Service, PNS Weekly Reports, February 17–21, 1986; Ricardo Pimentel, "Hispanic Legislators Stumble On Path to Wielding Power," *The Sacramento Bee,* Sunday, March 30, 1986, n.p.
12. See Rodolfo O. de la Garza and Robert R. Brischetto, *The Mexican American Electorate Series* (San Antonio, TX: Southwest Voter Registration Education Project and the Hispanic Population Studies Program of The Center for Mexican American Studies, The University of Texas at Austin), especially Occasional Papers No. 2 (1983) and No. 5 (1985); Robert R. Brischetto, "Hispanics in the 1984 Texas Presidential Election: An Analysis of Their Votes and Their Views," Southwest Voter Registration Education Project Report, November 28, 1984; and Midwest Voter Registration Education Project, *The Hispanic Vote: The November, 1984 General Election, A Comprehensive Analysis; The Midwest* (Columbus, OH: Midwest Voter Registration Education Project, March, 1985).
13. Harry Pachón, Director, National Association of Latino Elected and Appointed Officials (NALED), *1984 National Roster of Hispanic Elected Officials* (Washington D.C.: NALED Education Fund, 1984).
14. García, "Chicano Political Development," p. 10.
15. *Ibid.,* p. 11, and Pachón, *1984 National Roster of Hispanic Elected Officials,* pp. xi, xiii.
16. García, "Chicano Political Development," p. 11.

17. William C. Velasquez, Executive Director, Southwest Voter Registration Education Project, "Chicano Politics," public presentation, Colorado College, Colorado Springs, Colorado, May, 1982.

18. Data from a survey of political attitudes among Mexican Americans and Anglos in San Antonio, Texas indicate that a significant number of both groups agree with the statement, "Sometimes politics and government seem so complicated that a person like me can't really understand what is going on." Seventy percent of the Mexican Americans in the survey agreed with this statement compared to sixty-four percent of the Anglos. The difference between these percentages was not statistically significant. Robert R. Brischetto and Rodolfo O. de la Garza, *The Mexican American Electorate: Political Opinions and Behavior Across Cultures in San Antonio,* Occasional Paper No. 5 (Austin, TX: Southwest Voter Registration Education Project and the Hispanic Population Studies Program of The Center for Mexican American Studies, The University of Texas at Austin, 1985), pp. 14–15.

19. García, "Chicano Political Development," p. 11. The NALEO report finds a high correlation between Latino officeholders and constituencies in which Latinos comprise over 40% of the population. Pachón, *1984 National Roster of Hispanic Elected Officials,* p. xiv.

20. Christine Marie Sierra, "Surveying the Latina Political Landscape," The National Network of Hispanic Women, *Intercambios Femeniles,* Vol. 2, No. 3, Autumn, 1984, p. 1.

21. Pachón reports than in 1985, only 9% of all elected offices throughout the country were held by women. Pachón, *1984 National Roster of Hispanic Elected Officials,* p. xii.

22. Anglo-American methods of political domination, exclusion, and marginalization of the Mexican origin population in the Southwest are well documented. For an overview of these issues, see Christine M. Sierra, "Chicano Political Development: Historical Considerations," in *Chicano Studies: A Multidisciplinary Approach,* ed. Eugene García, Francisco Lomeli, and Isidro Ortiz (New York: Teachers College Press, Teachers College, Columbia University, 1984), pp. 79–98; and F. Chris García and Rudolph O. de la Garza, *The Chicano Political Experience: Three Perspectives* (North Scituate, MA: Duxbury Press, 1977).

23. Chicano scholars and organizations have begun to concern themselves with Mexican-born resident aliens and the reasons for their low rates of naturalization. See John A. García, "Political Integration of Mexican Immigrants: Explorations into the Naturalization Process," *International Migration Review* 15 (1981): 608–625; John A. García and Rodolfo O. de la Garza, "Mobilizing the Mexican Immigrant: The Role of Mexican-American Organizations," *The Western Political Quarterly* 38 (December 1985): 551–5l64; *NALEO National Report,* Vol. 5, No. 4, June, 1985, p. 6.

24. For a review of pertinent studies on American women, see Marianne Githens and Jewel L. Prestage, eds., *A Portrait of Marginality: The Political Behavior of the American Woman* (New York: D. McKay Company, 1977). Factors of race and class also distinguish the Chicana political experience from that of American women in general. Scholarship on Chicana electoral participation is virtually nonexistent. However, some important work focuses on Chicana organizational activity and additional concerns that have implications for Chicana politics. See, especially, Theresa Aragon de Valdez, "Organizing as a Political Tool for the Chicana," *Frontiers: A Journal of Women Studies* 5 (Summer 1980): 7–13; Magdalena Mora and Adelaida del Castillo, eds., *Mexican Women in the United States: Struggles Past and Present* (Los Angeles, CA: Chicano Studies Research Center, The University of California, Los Angeles, 1980); and Teresa Cordova, *et al.,* eds. *Chicana Voices: Intersections of Class, Race, and Gender* (Austin, TX: Center for Mexican American Studies, The University of Texas at Austin, 1986).

25. Assemblywoman Gloria Molina, "Chicanas and Double Jeopardy," roundtable discussion, Annual Meeting of the Western Political Science Association, Sacramento, California, April 12, 1984; Richard Santillán, "Latinas and Politics: A Case Study of Gloria Molina," paper presented at the 12th Annual Meeting of the National Associa-

tion for Chicano Studies, The University of Texas at Austin, Austin, Texas, March 8–10, 1984.

26. The work of political theorist Hanna Pitkin provides the essential framework for scholars in urban and Black politics in their evaluation of minority group representation. See Ira Katznelson, *Black Men, White Cities: Race, Politics, and Migration in the United States, 1900–30, and Britain, 1948–68* (Chicago: University of Chicago Press, 1976) for an excellent application of Pitkin's now classic typology of representation. Black political scientists have also increasingly focused on the role of Black elected officials as advocates for Black community interests. A useful bibliography is presented in Hanes Walton, Jr., "The Recent Literature on Black Politics," *PS* 18 (Fall 1985): 769–780. Also particularly useful is Michael B. Preston, Lenneal J. Henderson, Jr., and Paul Puryear, eds., *The New Black Politics: The Search for Political Power* (New York: Longman, 1982).

27. Rufus P. Browning, Dale Rogers Marshall, and David H. Tabb, *Protest Is Not Enough: The Struggle of Blacks and Hispanics for Equality in Urban Politics* (Berkeley, CA: University of California Press, 1984).

28. Southwest Voter Registration Education Project (SVREP) in cooperation with The Center on Budget and Policy Priorities, "Growing Problems in a Growing Community: A Series of Short Reports on Poverty, Unemployment and the Impact of Recent Budget and Tax Policies on Hispanics in the United States," 1984, Report #1, October, 1984, pp. 1, 4.

29. National Association of Latino Elected and Appointed Officials, *NALEO National Report*, Vol. 5, No. 1, September-October, 1984, p. 5.

30. SVREP, "Growing Problems in a Growing Community," Report #2, n.d., p. 1.

31. John L. Palmer and Isabel V. Sawhill, eds. *The Reagan Record: An Assessment of America's Changing Domestic Priorities* (Cambridge, MA: Ballinger Publishing Company, 1984). Findings from the Congressional Budget Office study are summarized in SVREP, "Growing Problems in a Growing Community."

32. SVREP, "Growing Problems in a Growing Community," Report #2, n.d., p. 3.

33. The data cited here are from surveys of Mexican American political attitudes in selected cities in the Southwest and Midwest. While not national in scope, these surveys, individually and collectively, provide some of the best data on Mexican American opinion to date. Rodolfo O. de la Garza and Robert R. Brischetto, with the assistance of David Vaughan, *The Mexican American Electorate: Information Sources and Policy Orientations*, Occasional Paper No. 2 (San Antonio, TX: Southwest Voter Registration Education Project and the Hispanic Population Studies Program of The Center for Mexican American Studies, The University of Texas at Austin, 1983), pp. 8–10; Robert R. Brischetto, "Hispanics in the 1984 Texas Presidential Election: An Analysis of Their Votes and Their Views," Southwest Voter Registration Education Project Report, November 28, 1984, pp. 7–9; Midwest Voter Registration Education Project, *The Hispanic Vote: The November, 1984 General Election, A Comprehensive Analysis: The Midwest* (Columbus, OH: Midwest Voter Registration Education Project, March, 1985), pp. 57–58. The latter two studies present data on Mexican American voters only.

34. *Ibid.* The questions asked of respondents vary slightly among the studies cited.

35. Brischetto, "Hispanics in the 1984 Texas Presidential Election," p. 8; Midwest Voter Registration Education Project, *The Hispanic Vote*, pp. 58–59.

36. De la Garza and Brischetto, *The Mexican American Electorate*, Occasional Paper No. 2, pp. 9–10.

37. National opinion and voting surveys usually include such a small sample of Hispanic respondents that the findings vary substantially and are subject to a wide margin of error. A lack of systematic and reliable data on the Latino population persists as a cause for concern.

38. Unlike the national network surveys, these data offer more in-depth analysis of Latino voting patterns. However, the surveys on which these findings are based differ in their degree of reliability due to variations in sampling procedures. Also, they are limited in their scope. Thus, generalizations from these findings must necessarily remain tentative and *suggestive* of national trends. Findings are summarized in Robert R. Brischetto,

"Latinos in the 1984 Election Exit Polls: Some Findings and Some Methodological Lessons," paper presented at Conference, "Ignored Voices: Public Opinion Polls and the Latino Community," The Center for Mexican American Studies, The University of Texas at Austin, October 19, 1985.

39. *Ibid.*, pp. 13–14.
40. Midwest Voter Registration Education Project, *The Hispanic Vote*, p. 55.
41. John Lasseville, pollster for the Spanish International Network (SIN), quoted in Jessica Lee, "Analysts Say Hispanic Vote Will Be Important in Close Race," *The El Paso Times,* October 7, 1984, n.p.
42. Brischetto, "Latinos in the 1984 Election Exit Polls," pp. 8, 12–13.
43. Brischetto, "Hispanics in the 1984 Texas Presidential Election."
44. Shortly before the 1984 presidential election, pollster George Gallup, Jr. noted that women had consistently given President Reagan lower approval ratings than men since he assumed office in 1981. Nevertheless, a majority of women voted for Reagan in 1984, but they did so to a lesser extent than men (55% vs. 64% respectively according to the Gallup poll). George Gallup, Jr., "Reagan's Approval Rating Remarkably Stable for 9 Months," *The Colorado Springs Gazette Telegraph,* August 5, 1984, p. C-3, and George Gallup, Jr., "Shift in Voting Patterns Found in Election Sweep," *The Colorado Springs Gazette Telegraph,* Friday, November 9, 1984, p. A-10. A national survey of Puerto Rican "opinion leaders" indicated overwhelming disapproval of President Reagan among men and women. However, Puerto Rican women showed slightly more disapproval than the men of Reagan's policies, especially in the area of foreign affairs. The Puerto Rican survey was conducted prior to the 1984 election. Data on Puerto Rican voting by gender is unavailable. Institute for Puerto Rican Policy, Inc., *NPROS, Puerto Ricans and the 1984 Presidential Race: A Report on the First National Puerto Rican Opinion Survey (NPROS) of the National Puerto Rican Policy Network,* March 1984, pp. 8, 11.
45. Brischetto, "Hispanics in the 1984 Texas Presidential Election," pp. 2–3.
46. De la Garza and Brischetto, *The Mexican American Electorate,* Occasional Paper No. 2, p. 26, and De la Garza, Brischetto, and Janet Weaver, *The Mexican American Electorate: An Explanation of Their Opinions and Behavior,* Occasional Paper No. 4 (San Antonio, TX: Southwest Voter Registration Education Project and the Hispanic Population Studies Program of The Center for Mexican American Studies, The University of Texas at Austin, 1984), pp. 9–10.
47. García, "Chicano Political Development," p. 17.
48. Thomas B. Edsall, "Liberals' Get-Out-the-Vote Turned Into Get Out Your Knives," *The Washington Post National Weekly Edition,* November 5, 1984, p. 23.
49. Raul Yzaguirre, Executive Director, National Council of La Raza, Washington, D.C. to Congressman Kent Hance, U.S. House of Representatives, May 17, 1984.
50. James Jennings, "Boston: Blacks and Progressive Politics," in *The New Black Vote,* ed. Rod Bush (San Francisco, CA: Synthesis Publications, 1984), p. 211.
51. Manning Marable, "Foreword," in *The New Black Vote,* p. 8.
52. *Ibid.*
53. Paul Taylor, " '88 'Underdog' Jackson Sharpens Political Bite," *The Washington Post,* Wednesday, April 16, 1986, p. A-3, and Taylor, "Jackson Declares a 'New Majority'," lThe Washington Post, Friday, April 19, 1986, p. A-12.
54. *Latinos in Metropolitan Chicago: A Study of Housing and Employment,* Monograph No. 6 (Chicago, IL: The Latino Institute, 1983), pp. 22–23.
55. Abdul Alkalimat and Doug Gills, "Chicago: Black Power vs. Racism, Harold Washington Becomes Mayor," in *The New Black Vote,* pp. 100–101.
56. *Ibid.*, pp. 150–151.
57. *Ibid.*, pp. 148–149.
58. *Ibid.*, pp. 103, 114–115, 151.
59. María Torres, Executive Director of the Mayor's Advisory Commission on Latino Affairs, public presentation, Chicago, Illinois, February 23, 1984. Also see the Alkalimat and Gills study of hindrances and successes to Latino/Black coalition building.

60. Latino groups voted for Washington in the following percentages: Puerto Ricans, 79%, Mexican Americans, 68%, and Cubans, 52%. Alkalimat and Gills, ''Chicago,'' p. 150/

61. María Torres, public presentation, February 23, 1984.

62. Joseph Daniel Sekul, ''The C.O.P.S. Story: A Case Study of Successful Collective Action,'' unpublished Ph.D. dissertation, The University of Texas at Austin, December, 1984.

HACIA UNA TEORÍA PARA LA LIBERACIÓN DE LA MUJER

Sylvia S. Lizárraga

ABSTRACT

Primeros apuntes en la delineación de un proceso teórico para la liberación de la mujer que tome en cuenta los factores de clase, raza y sexo. Se discuten las diferencias existentes en la situación de la mujer de raza minoritaria y de la clase trabajadora en los Estados Unidos y la situación de la mujer norteamericana, descendiente de europeos, de clase media. Se consideran las similaridades entre las mujeres y las diferencias dentro de las similaridades debido a la clase social y a la raza. Al examinar las diferencias de los intereses y las necesidades de las mujeres en su vida cotidiana, en sus experiencias como reproductoras, en la crianza de los hijos, en el consumo, en el trabajo doméstico y en el control sobre su vida se demuestra la necesidad de una toma de conciencia tri-dimensional, de clase, de raza y de sexo, si se desea lograr una verdadera igualdad para la mujer.

Para empezar a formular una teoría para la liberación de la mujer tenemos primero que estudiar las diferencias y similaridades de las mujeres según su situación histórica. La lucha por los derechos de la mujer se ha concebido, elaborado y actuado de manera distinta en diferentes partes del globo de acuerdo a la situacíon social y económica que las rige. Si tomamos, por ejemplo, el feminismo de la mujer del tercer mundo y el de la mujer norteamericana vemos que este feminismo es diferente desde su percepción.

Como yo lo comprendo, la diferencia estriba en que la lucha de la mujer del tercer mundo está bien definida dentro de un contexto histórico de lucha de clases—una lucha paralela de liberación de la ideología patriarcal así como de la liberación política, económica y sociológica en sus países. Y aquí hablo de la lucha de Domitila en Bolivia, de Rigoberta en Guatemala, de Luisa Amanda y sus seguidoras en Nicaragua. Para todas ellas no tiene sentido una lucha sólo por la liberación de la mujer sin que ésta esté acompañada de la liberación total del hombre.

En la arena en que se desarrolla esta lucha, la mujer del tercer mundo que ha llegado a adquirir una conciencia clara de su situación y de las causas de esa situación sabe que no puede separar estos terrenos. Sabe que no se puede alcanzar una sin la otra y su frente de batalla incluye a las dos.

La mujer feminista militante del tercer mundo por nececidad histórica está involucrada en las dos militancias. Está en contra de la ideología patriarcal impuesta y en contra del sistema económico que explota, emascula, distorsiona las identidades y hace de todos los habitantes de sus países, súbditos de un poder extranjero. Por esas razones no puede separar esas luchas, tan necesaria es la una como la otra para la liberación total, tanto de la mujer como del hombre.

La mujer norteamericana que lucha dentro del movimiento feminista ha tenido otra trayectoria histórica. No ha tenido, por lo menos en los últimos 200 años, que enfrentarse a una dominación extranjera. No ha tenido que unir sus esfuerzos con los del hombre en una militancia por liberación económica. Sus esfuerzos han sido siempre dentro de una lucha en contra de la ideología patriarcal, por una reivindicación de sus derechos civiles, así como también de sus derechos justos como ser humano.

En esta lucha, la mujer norteamericana, en su mayoría de la clase media, ha sido hasta hoy el paladín de todas las mujeres del mundo occidental y en similares circunstancias económicas, que la ven, en muchos casos, como ya emancipada.

Pero nosotras, las mujeres que vivimos en este país y que somos descendientes de personas originarias del tercer mundo, vemos que, si bien la mujer norteamericana ha alcanzado logros considerables, está aún muy lejos de su emancipación. Tanto en el terreno económico y político como en el ideológico, la mujer norteamericana en su mayoría está dominada por el hombre y sus instituciones, está escasamente representada en las jerarquías profesionales y en la vida social y política.

La mujer norteamericana aún gana sólo 60¢ por cada dólar que gana el hombre, aún trabaja más horas para ganar esa cantidad, aún tiene que soportar la hostigación sexual dentro y fuera del trabajo y aún, en muchos casos, está subordinada a los preceptos de la ideología patriarcal. Esta subordinación se manifiesta en los grupos de mujeres militantes en contra del aborto, y en los efectos producidos por los signos que recibimos por los medios de comunicación con la publicidad comercial y otros mensajes.

No hablo aquí de la dominación del hombre que se manifiesta en la forma cruda del machismo vulgar: de ese hombre que somete a la mujer ya sea por medio de gritos, golpes, o por temor a la seguridad personal, usando el estandard doble con las infidelidades, o abusando de la debilidad física con la violación sexual, manifestaciones todas éstas que sabemos son comunes en la sociedad norteamericana (no son los mexicanos los dueños exclusivos del machismo vulgar como se nos quiere hacer creer). De lo que hablo es del machismo más sofisticado, más sutil, el cual subordina a una mujer que aparentemente se presenta como íntegra y vocaliza como una marioneta lo que intuye agradará a sus superiores varones. Este es un machismo internalizado y son pocas las que se han liberado de él. Ya sea que estas mujeres estén obrando bajo una falsa conciencia o no, no importa, porque lo cierto es que están contribuyendo a la perpetuación de la ideología patriarcal. Aun cuando estén obrando por sus propios intereses, posición, prestigio, fama, esos intereses quedan supeditados a los intereses de los hombres y sus instituciones económicas.

En el otro lado del feminismo norteamericano, se encuentra la mujer feminista socialista. Aunque estas mujeres en realidad son pocas, sobresalen por su compromiso con los movimientos de liberación económica y política tanto en Estados Unidos como en los países del tercer mundo.

Dentro de Estados Unidos la mujer feminista socialista lucha por la reivindicación de los derechos de la mujer y trata de unir teóricamente dos vertientes ideológicas distintas: la de la mujer radical que ve al hombre como innecesario, o sea, la de las seguidoras de la autora de *La dialéctica sexual,* Shulamith Firestone, y la de la mujer que ve la necesidad de un cambio en la estructura económica de este país. De esta manera se podrá incluir a la mujer de la clase trabajadora en la liberación.

Como yo considero que la mujer chicana, la afro-americana, la puertorriqueña, la asiático-americana, que viven en este país, pertenecen en su mayoría a la clase trabajadora, he estudiado las teorías que expone la mujer feminista socialista norteamericana, y he encontrado, aun entre las más brillantes expositoras, una falta de comprensión de la situación de la mujer de raza minoritaria y de la clase trabajadora de este país.

No es a ellas, en toda justicia, a las que les toca desarrollar teorías para nuestra liberación. Es a nosotras, las que conocemos nuestra situación, nuestra circunstancia histórica, las que tenemos que estudiar, analizar y empezar ese proceso teórico. Es con ese fin, para empezar ese proceso teórico, que el siguiente análisis está hecho.

LA MUJER Y EL CAMBIO SOCIAL

Para la mujer de la clase trabajadora que vive en Estados Unidos, ya sea blanca, o de una raza minoritaria, el cambio del sistema económico tiene tanta prioridad como el cambio en la estructura patriarcal. Ella sufre opresión y explotación originadas por estas dos estructuras. Tiene que enfrentarse, por lo tanto, a las necesidades implícitas en la ejecución de ese cambio.

En primer lugar, hay que considerar que una lucha en contra del sistema económico, una revolución efectiva para cambiar la sociedad, no puede excluir al elemento masculino. Toda la clase trabajadora, hombres y mujeres, tendrían que unirse a lose miembros de las capas medias que están conscientes de la necesidad de un cambio.

En segundo lugar, la lucha feminista, basada en lo que las mujeres comparten en común debe tener lugar simultáneamente con la lucha de clases. Dentro de lo que las mujeres comparten en común se encuentra la asignación de la misma condición social del esposo o padre y la discriminación sexual en todos los niveles sociales donde hay relaciones entre mujeres y hombres. Y es aquí, desde el principio, que descubrimos que se abren los caminos. La condición social asignada varía según la clase así como también el grado de opresión.

Si bien es cierto que la opresión de la mujer en general y su falta de poder respecto al hombre son características que unirían a todas las mujeres, ¿hasta qué punto llegaría esta solidaridad?, ¿qué podríamos esperar del movimiento feminista de la clase media cuando la lucha se libraría en su propio suelo y no en un país remoto?, ¿cuáles son las diferencias de la vida cotidiana entre la mujer de la clase media y la de la clase trabajadora?, ¿cuáles son las diferencias entre sus experiencias en las actividades de reproducción, crianza de los hijos, consumo y trabajo doméstico?, ¿qué similaridades hay respecto a la libertad, autonomía y control sobre su vida entre las mujeres de la clase media y las de la clase trabajadora?

Es importante reconocer estas diferencias y similaridades de la vida de las mujeres en las diferentes clases sociales si queremos hacer un análisis de la realidad con la intención de cambiarla, sobre todo si queremos unir en la lucha a todas las mujeres en un movimiento feminista. Sabemos que las dos comparten la discriminación de la condición social. Pero la mujer de la clase trabajadora tiene además las desventajas propias de su clase, carece de los privilegios materiales que la mujer de clase media disfruta y que le proporcionan una vida más fácil, con más comodidad. La vida de esta última es más fácil porque tiene una casa más cómoda, en un mejor distrito, con muchos cuartos que le permiten ciertos momentos de privacía (y no estoy comparando a quí las dificultades y sufrimientos de las personas en los estratos más necesitados como son los hacinamientos de los indocumentados que viven tres y cuatro familias en una sola casa). Simplemente comparo las desventajas y los privilegios de una vivienda en un barrio pobre y una casa en un distrito residencial.

La mujer de la clase media en Estados Unidos tiene un coche para desempeñar su trabajo de consumidora que le hace la vida más cómoda. Ir a traer lo necesario para la familia en coche es diferente de tener que caminar y venir cargada con los abastecimientos. Eso, sin agregar la preocupación de tener que estirar el dinero, operación que causa un "stress" particular en la mujer trabajadora especialmente si es madre de familia. Esta preocupación se agudiza en las madres de la clase trabajadora por lo numeroso de sus hijos. (Es bien sabido que mientras más alta la posición de clase de las mujeres es menor el número de hijos que engendra).

En su trabajo como reproductora, la vida de la mujer de clase media es más confortable que la de la mujer que tiene que salir a trabajar. No es lo mismo estar en casa con los malestares propios del embarazo que tener que trabajar durante el embarazo, actividad en muchos casos imprescindible para la supervivencia. Esto sucede muy especialmente en los últimos tiempos cuando un sueldo no es suficiente para las necesidades básicas.

En la crianza de los hijos, la posición social también marca las diferencias. Se pueden costear guarderías para proporcionar más horas de descanso a la mujer o para desarrollar su potencial creativo. (Actividad prohibitiva para la mujer de la clase trabajadora. Se lleva a los niños a las guarderías sólo para poder trabajar). Además los mejores barrios tienen por supuesto mejores escuelas y lugares de recreación para los niños. Esta diferencia contribuye al proceso de perpetuación del estatus-quo de la sociedad, al ciclo que se establece de generación en generación debido al tipo de recreación y al medio ambiente. Bajo estas circunstancias, cada vez es más fácil la vida para los futuros hombres y mujeres de la clase media y cada vez les es más difícil salir de la pobreza y de sus consecuentes trastornos sociales a los niños y niñas de la clase trabajadora.

En el cuidado y mantenimiento del hogar, la vida de la mujer de la clase media se puede sobrellevar mejor que la de la mujer trabajadora porque tiene, o bien una trabajadora doméstica pagada o la ayuda de los aparatos electro-domésticos para aminorar un poco su trabajo. Estos aparatos los puede reemplazar fácilmente cuando ya no funcionen o les puede dar el servicio técnico necesario para que se conserven en buenas condiciones. Con esto se acortan las horas de trabajo embrutecedor.

En cuanto a la libertad, autonomía o control sobre su vida tanto la mujer de la clase media como la de la clase trabajadora comparten la misma situación—carecen en absoluto de esas características. (Pero no estoy tan segura que un hombre de la clase trabajadora las tenga tampoco). La mujer soltera de la clase trabajadora, si bien podría decirse que tiene más autonomía y control sobre su vida que la mujer de clase media casada, en realidad es muy poca. No tiene la libertad do no trabajar. En el trabajo, esta mujer sufre la explotación a la que es sometido todo trabajador y, encima de eso, tiene que soportar el hostigamiento sexual muchas veces ofensivo; además, sufre como toda mujer en el mercado laboral, de la desigualdad de salarios.

Si la mujer es madre soltera entonces su situación es mucho peor. Todas las responsabilidades del hogar, tanto económicas como sociales, recaen en ella. La crianza de los hijos se puede convertir en una verdadera pesadilla si no tiene parientes cercanos que le ayuden con el cuidado de los pequeños en las horas que tiene que salir a trabajar para la supervivencia.

Empezando a conocer estas diferencias y similaridades de la vida cotidiana de la mujer de las diferentes clases sociales nos ayudaría a ver la magnitud del problema. Reconocemos que la opresión de la mujer y su falta de poder con respecto al hombre son categorías que atraviesan las clases sociales. Sabemos que como mujeres compartimos la discriminación sexual que se deriva de los roles particulares asignados por el patriarcado. Pero pensamos que una organización de mujeres interclasista tendría muchas dificultades. La mujer de la clase media tendría como prioridad cambiar el sistema patriarcal. Para esa lucha, la mujer de la clase trabajadora se uniría a la mujer de la clase media porque tienen intereses en común. Pero para cambiar la vida cotidiana de la mujer de la clase trabajadora en Estados Unidos, ya sea blanca o de una raza minoritaria, el cambio del sistema económico tiene tanta prioridad como el cambio en la estructura patriarcal. A esa lucha sería muy difícil reclutar a una mujer que goza de privilegios económicos, materiales, tangibles. En el terreno económico los intereses son opuestos. ¿Quién desearía arriesgar su posición de bienestar, sus comodidades físicas y sus privilegios para solidarizarse con una organización que tiene como meta precisamente destruir su posición privilegiada? Serían muy pocas las mujeres que harían traición a su clase y se unirían a esta causa. No es imposible, desde luego, y ya se ha hecho en todas las revoluciones; pero sí es indispensable si se considera que el cambio del sistema económico es tan necesario como el patriarcal.

La toma de conciencia de clase de la mujer precisamente la coloca en campos opuestos según la clase a la que pertenezca. Esto es ya un problema inmenso para conseguir una unión. Ahora, si añadimos el problema de la diferencia de razas en la sociedad americana, que es un factor fundamental en un análisis completo de la sociedad en que vivimos, podemos empezar a ver el panorama social que enfrentamos. Para comprender la opresión de la mujer chicana, negra, india o asiática, hay que comprender todo el proceso social del cual es parte.

La situación de la mujer de la clase trabajadora y de diferente raza que la dominante se complica aún más cuando incluimos en su estudio este factor fundamental. Esta mujer, no sólo sufre la opresión como mujer que todas, por parejo sufren, sino también la extrema explotación en el mercado laboral, aparte de la injuria psicológica a causa de la discriminación particular por ser de una raza diferente. Vilipendio que sufre por igual de hombres y mujeres de origen europeo de todas las clases sociales.

Así como la opresión de la mujer en general está enraizada en algo más que su posición de clase—el orden sexual jerárquico de la sociedad, así también, la opresión de la mujer de diferente raza está enraizada en algo más que su posición de clase y su condición de ser mujer—el orden racial de la sociedad. En otras palabras, el racismo existente en Estados Unidos institucionalizado en todas las relaciones sociales es parte de su opresión.

El racismo co-existe con el capitalismo a través de una red ideológica que estructura este orden racial de la sociedad. Este orden se origina no sólo de interpretaciones ideológicas sino también políticas de las diferencias raciales (biológicas). El hecho de que la pigmentación de la piel sea diferente se ha usado ideológica y políticamente para una formulación particular de opresión y explotación.

La ideología racista ha creado estereotipos, mitos, e ideas que asignan una ubicación de inferioridad a las personas de razas diferentes a las europeas. Esta ubicación de inferioridad se utiliza para justificar su explotación extrema en el sistema capitalista. Son las personas de raza diferente las que ocupan los puestos más despreciados y más severos en donde en ocasiones reciben un trato inhumano (los trabajadores agrícolas migratorios, por ejemplo). Son ellas las que sufren las fluctuaciones del sistema capitalista, las que figuran en las altas cifras del desempleo y del subempleo; son las últimas en emplearse y las primeras en despedirse. La supremacía de la raza está institucionalizada en todos los organismos sociales y culturales. En los medios de comunicación se usan imágenes para fortalecer los estereotipos. Se enfatiza lo emocional e irracional como sus características raciales naturales. En la educación son practicamente excluídas. Las personas de raza diferente son las que ocupan los índices más bajos de participación. Y dentro de esos índices es la mujer la que está menos representada.

La ideología racista, sexista y clasista juega, pues, un papel importante en la definición de la posición que ocupa la mujer chicana, negra, india o asiática en la estructura de clases de esta sociedad. Esta ideología es el producto de las relaciones sociales concretas. Es la manera en que esas relaciones de clase, de sexo y de raza se experimentan, se legitimizan y se perpetúan.

Así como los sistemas vigentes crean las ideologías necesarias para su mantenimiento, así también las ideologías tienen impacto en la realidad y la alteran. En nadie se ve tan claro en esta sociedad como en la mujer de la clase trabajadora y de raza que no desciende de los europeos, los obstáculos que en ocasiones se transforman en barreras infranqueables y que le imposibilitan escapar de esas relaciones sociales; como la encierran, la atrapan, debido a la necesidad material.

La toma de conciencia de clase, de raza y de sexo es crucial para desarrollar su potencial revolucionario. Las presiones ideológicas que impiden su realización son tan poderosas que vuelven realidad lo imaginario e imaginaria la realidad. Los años, siglos, de discriminación sexual, racial y clasista no han pasado en vano, han hecho estragos en la psiquis de la mujer de raza diferente a la dominante. Los casos de sumisión pasiva extrema, de aceptación de la subordinación sin protestar, de la pérdida de identidad que sufren muchas mujeres pueden rastrearse tanto a las presiones ideológicas como a las condiciones materiales.

En esta pérdida de identidad en la que el medio ambiente las obliga a negarse a sí mismas, a negar su cultura y su historia, viven muchas mujeres en una especie de limbo en el que no se es ni una cosa ni la otra. Algunas mujeres que se han integrado al movimiento chicano, negro, indio o asiático, y que han estudiado sus raíces culturales e históricas, así como también las condiciones materiales que causan este fenómeno, han logrado superarlo. Pero no son la mayoría de las mujeres de raza diferente a la dominante en Estados Unidos.

El efecto destructor más vitriólico en la psiquis de la mujer por medio de estas presiones ideológicas es el de odiarse a sí misma por el color de la piel o por el rasgo de los ojos. Los efectos de la discriminación sexual hacen a la mujer una víctima ya sea consciente o inconsciente de su situación. Pero la discriminación racista hace a la mujer víctima y verdugo de sí misma al mismo tiempo. En los casos de aceptación extrema, de internalización de la ideología racista, se produce odio de la mujer hacia sí misma.

Estas consecuencias psicológicas nefastas, así como la explotación extrema, hacen imperativa la erradicación de la ideología racista y su consideración como una de las prioridades al mismo nivel que la discriminación sexual en la lucha por la igualdad.

Por otra parte, debido a este factor racial, en los casos en que la mujer ha logrado una comprensión de la discriminación sexual en la sociedad capitalista, su situación se vuelve más problemática. Como tiene que tener alianzas de clase y de raza con los hombres, cualquier desviación de su subordinación, cualquier intento asertivo de emancipación, se puede calificar de separatismo, de traición que causaría divisiones en la lucha racial o de clases. Acusación que viene de la falta de comprensión de la situación de la mujer así como del temor de perder una estabilidad basada en los privilegios que se han tenido por tantos años.

Para lograr la igualdad de la mujer en todos los niveles, la toma de conciencia de hombres y mujeres tiene que ser tri-dimensional—de clase, de raza y de sexo. Esta será la única forma de efectuar un cambio total en el ordenamiento de la sociedad. No importa a qué raza o clase pertenezca cualquier persona, hombre o mujer, si se compromete en la lucha por un cambio social deberá estar consciente de la opresión a esos tres niveles. Así como los hombres comprometidos con la lucha de clases deben estar conscientes de la opresión sexual de la mujer, así también hombres y mujeres por igual, de cualquier raza que sean, deben estar conscientes de la opresión racial y empezar a analizar críticamente todas las situaciones de acuerdo con su conciencia social. Sólo así se logrará la unidad necesaria para efectuar el cambio total.

THE CHICANO MOVEMENT AND THE TREATY OF GUADALUPE HIDALGO

Richard Griswold del Castillo

ABSTRACT

In the 1960s the Chicano political movement revived an interest in the Treaty of Guadalupe Hidalgo, a nineteenth century document ending the Mexican War. Reies Tijerina's Alianza, Rudolfo "Corky" Gonzalez's Denver Crusade for Justice, and Richard Sanchez's Brown Berets all interpreted the treaty to justify a new era of political activism. Chicano activist-scholars such as Armando Rendon and Fernando Chacon Gomez also wrote about the treaty and helped disseminate its importance. The Treaty of Guadalupe Hidalgo thus became a key document in the Chicano struggle.

During the 1960s and 1970s Chicano political militants sought to focus world attention on the failed promises of the Treaty of Guadalupe Hidalgo. Beginning with an agrarian revolutionary movement in New Mexico and spreading to urban university campuses, the Chicano movement resurrected the Treaty of Guadalupe Hildalgo as a primary document in the struggle for social justice. An entire generation of Mexican Americans learned of the legal basis for reclaiming their lost homeland, Aztlán. The political aims of the Chicano movement, to gain representation and recognition, became an integral part of a historical interpretation of the meaning of the Mexican War and the treaty. A lasting legacy of the Chicano revolution was its fostering of a consciousness of the importance of history dating from 1848 and the Treaty of Guadalupe Hidalgo.

The Treaty of Guadalupe Hidalgo ended the war between Mexico and the United States in 1848. The most important provisions affecting Chicanos were contained in Articles 8 and 9 which guaranteed the protections of civil and property rights for Mexican citizens who were being annexed by the United States. Article 8 stipulated that the property rights of landholders who continued to live in Mexico after 1848 would be protected. Article 9 outlined the intention of the United States to give United States citizenship to those Mexican citizens who wanted it and that in the meantime they would be protected in the full enjoyment of their liberty and property. Another article protecting the validity of incomplete Mexican titles had been deleted from the orignal treaty by the United States Senate prior to its ratification. In its stead, the United States government had signed the Protocol of Querétaro affirming their intention to abide by the spirit of the treaty, to protect the rights of the Mexicans who were now going to be part of the United States. Knowledge about the treaty's provisions was not widespread prior to the 1960s. Only a handful of scholars had studied the treaty and it was hardly mentioned at all in the history textbooks used in the public schools. If Chicanos knew anything at all about the treaty it was usually that it was among the many broken promises of the Anglo Americans.

One of the first Chicano activists to provoke a reassessment of the treaty was Reies Lopez Tijerina. Originally a fundamentalist preacher from Texas, Tijerina became part of the struggle of the Hispanos of New Mexico to regain the community land grants that had been taken from them after 1848 in violation of the treaty. In 1959 and again in 1964 he traveled to Mexico City representing New Mexican land claimants to present memorials to the Mexican authorities, including the president of Mexico. Thousands of Hispanos whose families had lost their lands in violation of the terms of the treaty signed the petitions. Reies and the delegation asked that the government of Mexico demand that the United States fulfill the terms of the treaty, in particular those in Articles 8 and 9. On both occasions the Mexican government listened respectfully but did nothing.[1]

During the early 1960s Tijerina traveled throughout New Mexico organizing La Alianza Federal de Mercedes Libres. The purpose of the organization was "to organize and acquaint the heirs of all Spanish land-grants covered by the Guadalupe Hidalgo Treaty" with their rights.[2] This organization became the catalyst for a number of militant actions: the occupation of Kit Carson National Forest, the proclamation of the Republic of San Joaquin de Chama, the courthouse raid and shootout at Tierra Amarilla, a massive military manhunt for Tijerina and his followers, and lengthy legal battles. Forgotten or ignored in the sensational publicity surrounding Tijerina and the Alianza during the late 1960s was the fact that Alianza leaders justified their movement by historical and legal interpretations of the constitutions of New Mexico, the United States, and the Treaty of Guadalupe Hidalgo. Much like the American Indian Movement of the same period, the Alianza claimed that legitimate treaty rights had been violated and demanded compensation.

Tijerina's analysis of the land-grant question appeared in a booklet that the Alianza published and distributed throughout the Southwest.[3] Tijerina based his arguments for the reclamation of lost Hispano lands on two documents, the *Recopilacion de leyes de las Indias,* which had been the legal framework for the Spanish land-grants prior to the nineteenth century, and the Treaty of Guadalupe Hidalgo. He contended that the United States had violated Articles VIII and IX of the treaty which had guaranteed property and citizenship rights to Mexicans.

Ultimately Tijerina's claims were presented before the United States Supreme Court as a class action law suit in 1969. Denied a hearing two times, the case finally received, in 1970, a favorable recommendation for a hearing but was not presented probably due to a shortage in Tijerina's funding to pursue the issue (Tijerina et. al. v U.S.; 396 US 843; 396 US 990; and 396 US 922).

A few years later the legal and moral issues raised by Tijerina's Alianza movement influenced Senator Joseph Montoya of New Mexico to introduce a bill in the United States Senate. This bill (S68) proposed to create a Special Commission on Guadalupe Hidalgo Land Rights. Simultaneously Representative Manuel Lujan (New Mexico) introduced a similar bill in the House (HR 3595). Montoya proposed that the federal government establish a temporary commission that would review violations of property rights guaranteed in the treaty and make recommendations to Congress and the President regarding restitution. One of the first tasks of the commission would be to "make a comprehensive study of the provisions of the Treaty of Guadalupe Hidalgo" in order to determine violations of the treaty. Senator Montoya, by no means a political ally of Reies Tijerina, adopted what seemed to be a radical questioning of established land tenures in his home state. He justified his measure as a means of rectifying past injustices: "If certain lands have been wrongfully taken from people, we must make amends."[4] Montoya's bill reflected the degree to which the long and bitter history of land-grant conflict in New Mexico had emerged as an issue for federal concern.

Senator Montoya's bill died in the Insular and Interior Affairs Committee, as did a similar bill introduced the same year by Congressman Augustus Hawkins of California (HR 2207). Hawkins proposed that Congress establish a Community Land Grant Act targeted specifically at the villages of New Mexico. Like Montoya, he envisioned the establishment of a commission that would hear petitions from members of villages whose community land-grants had been lost through corruption or deceit. The commission was to have the power to "reconstitute the community land-grant" under the Laws of the Indies where it was consistent with the Constitution or state laws. Additionally the Hawkins bill provided for $10 million to finance the operations of the commission. This bill also died in committee. Unfortunately there are no records of the debate surrounding either Montoya's or Hawkin's bill in these committees. That these measures were defeated was not too surprising since any federal investigation into land tenure in New Mexico would be found to unsettle powerful commercial and speculative interests.

Nevertheless Congressional interest in investigating the violations of the Treaty's provisions continued. Throughout the 1970s at least three bills were introduced. In 1977 Representative Henry B. Gonzalez (Texas) introduced a resolution to create a special congressional committee "to investigate the legal, political, and diplomatic status of lands which were subject to grants from the King of Spain and the Government of Mexico prior to the acquisition of the American Southwest as a result of the Treaty of Guadalupe Hidalgo." In 1979 Representative Ronald V. Dellums (California) introduced a similar proposal, but a House committee rejected it. Finally, in 1979, as a result of lobbying by Reies Tijerina, the New Mexico legislature instructed its representatives to introduce legislation to establish a board of review to investigate the theft of communal lands in northern New Mexico.[5] This move, like others before it was killed by conservative interests in Congress. The motivation for the continued legistlative attempts to rectify the land-grant situation in New Mexico came primarily from increased public awareness and pressure originating from a revitalized Alianza movement. Again, the public records are silent on the debates surrounding these measures since each was quashed without a lengthy hearing.

Knowledge of the treaty and its violation was widespread among New Mexicans. Collectively they had been fighting for a return of their pueblo lands for more than a century. Millions of urban Chicanos, however, the sons and daughters of Mexican immigrants who had entered the United States 1910, had to be educated about the treaty. In the 1960s and 1970s this process took place in informal meetings, discussions, and rallies.

In the spring of 1968 urban and rural Chicano leaders found a common ground for dialog. Rudolfo "Corky" Gonzales, leader and organizer of the Denver Crusade for Justice, joined forces with Reies Tijerina to participate in the Poor People's

March on Washington, D.C. Together with other urban leaders they issued a joint statement entitled *We Demand*, listing the needs of Chicanos throughout the nation. These included bilingual education, adaquate housing, job development, more sensitive law enforcement, economic opportunities and agricultural reforms. The demand for agricultural reforms, inspired by Tijerina's struggle in New Mexico, called not only for a return of lands stolen from the pueblos in violation of the Treaty, but also for "compensation for taxes, legal costs, etc., which pueblo heirs spent trying to save their land."[6]

The Treaty of Guadalupe and its implications became a topic of discussion at the first Annual Youth Conference in Denver, Colorado, organized by Gonzales in 1969. Knowledge of the violation of the treaty became a driving force behind the final statement of the conference in "El Plan Espiritual de Aztlán," a document of Chicano solidarity and a declaration of independence.

During the 1970s surveys and critiques of the treaty and especially of Articles VIII and IX began to appear in the anthologies and books that publishers were producing to satisfy the demand for more printed materials dealing with Chicanos. One of the most popular of these was Armando Rendon's *Chicano Manifesto*. In the section of the book dealing with the treaty, Rendon summarized the prevalent view of the importance of the treaty: "The Treaty of Guadalupe Hidalgo is the most important document concerning Mexican Americans that exists."[7] The terms and spirit of the treaty, he said, had been systematically violated by the United States government. He called for Chicanos to become aware of the "exact processes by which the Treaty of Guadalupe Hidalgo was made meaningless over the past century and a half." Rendon had in mind a detailed documentary case that could be made against the federal government so that some kind of compensation could be exacted. He hinted that Chicanos could seek, as the American Indian tribes had, monetary settlements or even a return of territory to Mexico.[8] The realistic possibility of the latter taking place was nil. The prospect of a monetary settlement, however, did not, in the political atmosphere of the time, seem wholly impossible. For many militants of the 1970s the treaty became a historical basis for legitimizing their demands for social and economic justice as well as providing a cause for radical action.

The same year that Rendon's *Chicano Manifesto* appeared, the most dramatic attempt to publicize the importance of the treaty took place. In September 1972 the Brown Berets in California began a twenty-four-day "occupation" of Santa Catalina Island claiming that it had never been included in the original treaty and was thus still part of Mexico.

The Brown Berets were founded in 1967 by David Sanchez, a former chairman of the Los Angeles Mayor's Youth Council. Eventually the Berets would claim five thousand members nationwide. As an organization the Berets had as their goal the fulfillment of the ideals articulated in "El Plan Espiritual de Aztlan," namely to control or at least have a voice in the policies of major institutions in the barrio that affected Chicanos: the schools, police, welfare offices, and the immigration service. As an action-oriented militant organization, the Berets participated in and helped organize most of the major landmarks of the Chicano movement: the high-school "blowouts" and the Moratorium marches in East Los Angeles, (La Marcha and Caravana de la Reconquista) as well as other local actions in Southern California designed to raise public awareness of oppression and racism.

A particular interpretation of the meaning of the Treaty of Guadalupe Hidalgo influenced the Brown Beret's decision to stage a symbolic occupation of Santa Catalina Island. None of the nine channel islands off the coast of Southern California had been mentioned in the treaty as part of the territory ceded to the United States in 1848. According to popular beliefs in Mexico and in many barrios, the islands remained part of Mexico until the 1870s, when Benito Juarez, then president of Mexico, leased Catalina Island to Americans. Eventually Mr. Wrigley of the chewing-gum empire acquired the property. The lease which was to run for ninety-nine years, expired in 1970.[9] The true history of Catalina Island's title contradicted this folk history. On July 4, 1846, Pío Pico, the last Mexican governor of California granted the island of Catalina to Tomas Robbins. Robbins sold the island to Jose Maria Covarrubias of Santa Barbara in 1850 and Covarrubias sold it to Albert Roshard of San Francisco in 1853. Thereafter the title to the island is traceable up to William Wrigley Jr.'s purchase in 1919.[10] Athough the claim that Catalina had been leased from Mexico had no historical basis, the story reflected the need of the Mexicano and Chicano communities to keep alive the issue of the illegal seizure of their lands. The legend also reflected a real ambiguity in the Treaty of Guadalupe Hidalgo regarding the status of the off shore islands. This vagueness had been a source of sporadic public discussion in the 1950s and 60s.[11] On the other hand there were some legal experts in Mexico who were prepared to argue that the island could be reclaimed by Mexico. A partial basis for argument was the fact that governor Pico's grant of the island was made after the declaration of war and hence was considered invalid by both the U.S. and Mexican governments.[12] Late in the nineteenth century the Mexican government had considered making the ownership of the islands an international issue. In 1894 the United States asserted control over Clipperton Island (called Medanos or La Pasion by Mexico) a small island some one thousand miles off the coast of southern Mexico. Mexican newspapers claimed that this island was rightfully Mexico's and that the Catalina Islands should be "reclaimed" by the Mexican government in retaliation. The issue became an item for official private correspondance but soon died for lack of presidential support.[13]

Eighty years later the Brown Berets did not seriously believe that they could regain the island for Mexico. The real purpose of the occupation was to provide a forum for discussion of the problems confronting Mexican Americans arising from their colonized status.

After a week of isolation to plan the offensive against the island and to prevent police informants from telegraphing the group's moves, the Berets assembled 25 men and 1 woman in Avalon harbor on August 30, 1972. The next morning the citizens of the small town awoke to see a huge Mexican flag flying above them on a hill. The Beret contingent carried no arms but stood in formation, dressed in the Beret fashion with military gear. At first some residents, recalling folktales about the controversial title to the islands, thought they had been invaded by the Mexican Army.[14]

The mayor of Avalon, Raymond Rydell, a former vice-chancellor of the California State College system, had dealt with student militants during the 1960s. He encouraged the sheriff's department to use a low-key approach to the Beret encampment and to leave them alone as long as they caused no trouble. The vice-president of Santa Catalina Island Company was a Mexican American named Renton. He too advised the sheriffs to leave the Berets alone. To show his good will he sent the Beret contingent cold drinks and box lunches.[15] David Sanchez told the media that they were there to discuss social and political issues. "We want to discuss why the OD wards are filled with Mexicans, people of Mexican descent, dying from self-inflicted persecution. We want to discuss why there is violence in the streets with Mexican young people killing one another."[16]

The occupation lasted twenty-four days. During that time the Beret camp became something of a tourist attraction. The small Mexican-American population of the island helped provide food and drink for the Chicano demonstrators. Local restaurateur Mike Budd gave them a free meal at his restaurant. As the occupation stretched into weeks, the Berets had a chance to talk to some of the island's Chicano residents. Their message was that the United States was illegally occupying not just Catalina but all of Aztlán; the American Southwest was occupied Mexico. Mexican-Americans were a colonized people, victims of an unjust was of aggression.

The occupation of Catalina ended peacefully on September 23, when the city council decided to enforce a local camping ordinance and threatened jail unless the Berets abandoned their campground. The Berets left, vowing to return to occupy other islands at some future date and to engage in more legal research.[17] As it turned out, however, the Catalina occupation was the last organized action of the Brown Berets. A few weeks later their leader, David Sanchez, citing the pervasive presence of police informants within the organization announced that the Brown Berets had been disbanded.[18]

The Treaty of Guadalupe Hidalgo provided a basis for legitimizing the occupation of Catalina Island, the presentation of grievances and the dramatization of la causa. Compared to Tijerina and the Alianza's occupation of Kit Carson National Forest and the shootout at Tierra Amarilla, Catalina Island was a relatively minor incident. Nevertheless, the Santa Catalina occupation demonstrated the degree to which some Chicanos were willing to take militant action based on the historical violations of the Treaty of Guadalupe Hidalgo.

The only segment of American society that has kept alive the issues raised by this treaty is the Mexican-Americans. Thanks to popular movements of the 1960s and 1970s as well as the institutionalization of Chicano Studies classes in major universities, larger numbers of Chicanos have an idea of the significance of the treaty. More often than not, however, this familiarity does not go beyond a belief that the treaty guaranteed certain rights for Mexican Americans and that these rights have been violated.

Only a few Chicano scholars have attempted to go beyond this generalized view of the implications of the treaty. Perhaps the most detailed, scholarly, and realistic appraisal of the meaning of the treaty for Chicano rights appeared in 1978 as a doctoral dissertation by Fernando Chacon Gomez. Before Gomez no one had analyzed how the treaty influenced subsequent court cases involving Chicanos. This work was a conscious blending of the activism of the Chicano movement with scholarly training.

Gomez's main argument was that despite decades of "invisibility" and general neglect, the Treaty of Guadalupe Hidalgo had real legal implications for the present. He wanted to explore the treaty's legal history after 1848 to determine "to what extent it could be used to compel enforcement of contemporary civil rights." He analyzed the cultural and historical background of the legal battles that had been waged in the nineteenth and early twentieth centuries to secure property and civil rights for former Mexican citizens. On a case-by-case basis he pointed to the ethnocentric and racist basis of the arguments and decisions. Manifest Destiny, he concluded, had found its way into the courtroom. This was especially true in New Mexico where, because of the judge's ignorance of local tradition, "the century-old concept of flexibility of the common law may indeed have been 'bastardized'." Elsewhere in the United States judges relied on local precedent in making decisions. Not so in New Mexico. Thus, although the treaty was a "rights conferring document", in practical operation in the courts, it remained a dead letter. Chacon

Gomez concluded that the most viable avenues for redress were largely in the international arena, since the Supreme Court had consistently ruled against interpreting the Treaty of Guadalupe Hidalgo in a way that protected Chicano rights. A legal attack on the injustices and inequalities confronted by Chicanos, he thought, could best be pursued in international forums like the United Nations and the World Court.[18]

This approach is one that is currently being actively pursued by a handful of Chicano activists. The fact that the United Nations has granted the American Indians Native Peoples status as a Non-Government Organization (NGO) has encouraged some to actively pursue this avenue for Chicanos. If Chicanos were given NGO status then debate over issues would be more serious. A joint American Indian and Chicano conference on the Treaty of Guadalupe Hidalgo took place in Flagsaff, Arizona, in May 1986. If sufficient legal expertise is organized and focused on the violations of the treaty it may well prove to be an international issue within the United Nations or a cause championed by Mexico or other Latin American governments.

The Treaty of Guadalupe Hidalgo became a focal point for claims of social and economic justice during the activist sixties and seventies through militant action, popular books and scholarly studies. An important legacy of the Chicano movement was its fostering of a particular historical awareness. This was the view that the Southwest was really "occupied Mexico", and that Mexican Americans were a "colonized people" whose rights had been violated despite the guarantees of the treaty. Thus the Treaty of Guadalupe became an integral part of the Chicano desire to reclaim their lost land, Aztlán, the ancient homeland of the first Mexicans, the Aztecs.[19]

NOTES

1. Patricia Bell Blawis, *Ti,eriana and the Land Grants* (New York: International Publishers, 1970), p. 37; see also Richard Gardner, *Grito!: Reies Ti,erina and the New Mexican Land Grant Wars of 1967* (New York, San Francisco, Everston and London: Harper and Row Publishers, 1970) and Peter Nabokov, *Ti,erina and the Courthouse Raid* (Albuquerque: University of New Mexico Press, 1969); For Tijerina's own account of the trip and the Allianza see Reies Tijerina, *Mi lucha por tierra* (Mexico: Fondo de Cultura y Economia, 1978).
2. Richard Gardner, p. 96.
3. Reies Tijerina, *The Spanish Land Grant Question Examined* (Albuquerque: Alianza Federal, 1966).
4. *Congressional Record*, Vol. 21, p.t 1, January 15, 1975, pp. 321–322.
5. The summaries of these bills were provided by the Library of Congress as follows: HR2207, 94th Congress 1/28/75; HRES 585, 95th Congress 5/18/77; HRES 16, 96th Congress 1/15/79; *Albuquerque Journal*, March 16, 1979, 8:6.
6. Luis Valdez and Stan Steiner, eds., *Aztlán: An Anthology of Mexican American Literature*, "We Demand" (New York: Alfred A. Knopf, 1972), p. 220.
7. Armando Rendon, *Chicano Manifesto* (New York: Macmillan Publishing Co., 1972), p. 81.
8. Ibid., pp. 84–85.
9. Maria Blanco, "A Brief History About the Brown Beret National Organization," unpublished ms., November 10, 1975., pp. 4–6.
10. Adelaide Lefert Daron, *The Ranch that was Robbins': Santa Catalina Island, California* (Los Angeles: Arthur Clark Company, 1963), Ch. 6.
11. In Mexico the issue of the islands produced a masters thesis arguing that they were still part of Mexico; see J. Antonio Rosete Murgia, "El Tratado de Guadalupe y el problema de las islas catalina," (tesis, UNAM, 1957). Rosete Murgia recommended that Mexico reopen negotiations over the status of the Catalina islands under Article 21 of the Treaty of Guadalupe Hidalgo; See *Los Angeles Times*, August 31, 1972, for details of the intial occupation.
12. Luiz Zorrilla, *Historia de la relaciones entre Mexico y los Estados Unidos de America, 1800–1958*, 2 vols. (Mexico: Editorial Porrua, 1977), II: 85.
13. *LA Times*, August 31, 1972, I, 1:2.
14. *LA Times*, September 2, I 1:5.
15. *LA Times*, August 31, 1972, loc. cit.
16. *LA Times*, September 23, 1972, II 1:2.
17. Fernando Chacon Gomez, "The Intended and Actual Effects of Article VIII of the Treaty of Guadalupe Hidalgo: Mexican Treaty Rights Under International and Domestic Law," (Ph.D. diss., University of Michigan, 1977), p. 197.
18. See especially Rudolfo Acuña, *Occupied America: The Chicano's Struggle Toward Liberation*, 1st ed. (San Francisco: Canfield Press, 1972), pp. 27–30; most recently see the appraisal by John R. Chavez, *The Lost Land; The Chicano Image of the Southwest* (Albuquerque: University of New Mexico Press, 1984), pp. 129–155.

Part II

CULTURE

ASSIMILATION REVISITED

Renato Rosaldo

ABSTRACT

Chicano political demands that promote social mobility (such as affirmative action) raise a vexed question: can we improve our economic conditions only by losing our cultural identity? Does soci.l mobility always lead to assimilation? Are social mobility and assimilation the same thing? Arguably, assimilation has been poorly understood as a process. Rather than a linear trend, assimilation could be conceived as a heterogeneous contradictory phenomenon.

Assimilation has always been a vexed issue. Politically, the concept usually links cultural loss to economic betterment. It suggests, for example, that Chicanos who raise their incomes automatically lose their ethnic identity. Surely economic misery is not the only path to cultural vitality. In what follows I argue that processes of assimilation have been so poorly understood that the available literature cannot serve as a guide to political action.

All too often studies of assimilation assume the answers to questions that require investigation. Can one assume, for example, that assimilation moves in a straight line? Is it a linear homogeneous trend? Is it simply a function of social mobility? Can it reverse itself? Is all cultural change assimilation? Should cultural retention and the assertion of ethnic identity be separated? Are these processes so complex and contradictory that people can assimilate in certain respects, and assert their ethnic identity in other respects? These questions highlight certain unresolved conceptual muddles that could prove deblitating for assimilation models.

The term assimilation has a double meaning. It can refer either to structural or to cultural assimilation. Often called acculturation, cultural assimilation refers to degree of fluency, both narrowly with reference to language and more broadly in the skills required for minority group members to succeed in the majority group's formal institutions and informal social situations. Judged by the majority group's standards, those fully assimilated in a cultural sense speak properly, known how to behave, and have the education needed for the job at hand. Structural assimilation, in contrast, refers to the capacity of minorities to enter any available position in the dominant

This paper has benefitted from comments by Jose Limon, Mary Louise Pratt, and the faculty seminar at the Stanford Center for Chicano Research.

society. Depending on their talent and desire to apply it, those fully assimilated in a structural sense could in principle become anything, from street sweeper to president. In short, the term can refer either to personal identity (cultural assimilation) or equal opportunity (structural assimilation).

From a political perspective, assimilation has contradictory implications. For minority people, structural assimilation has long been advocated under the name of affirmative action or equal opportunity. Minority people's life chances should compare favorably with those of the majority population. They should have equal education, equal housing, and equal jobs, or at any rate a fair opportunity to achieve these goals. The other side of the coin, however, has been that affirmative action could bring a loss of ethnicity, both as personal identity and political voice. If structural assimilation automatically produced cultural assimilation, short-run economic victories could contain the seeds of ethnicity's destruction, thereby bringing long-run defeat to minority movements.

For majority people, comparable ambiguities abound. They can favor assimilation as either a conservative or a liberal stance. Conservatives see assimilation as a means of absorbing a threatening population. If assimilation fails, deportation appears to be the only alternative. On the other hand, liberals view assimilation as democratic and egalitarian. They contrast assimilation with systems of segregation and apartheid where minorities occupy only the lowest rung of the social ladder. Apparently, the same phenomenon can stimulate opposed political assessments, a mixed chorus of cheers and hisses.

Yet terminological ambiguities and contradictory perceptions of assimilation can also mask deeper problems of conceptual analysis. To put it bluntly, for all the heated debate the phenomenon of assimilation has been poorly understood. In attempting a deeper understanding, aggregate data analysis should be supplemented through circumstancial case studies that produce new questions and new understandings about how the process works.

In the broadest terms, three problems have proven stultifying in assimilation studies. First, rather than asking about agency, including, foremost among other things, social reproduction and mechanisms for cultural creativity, analysts have concentrated on the individual organism and its literal biological reproduction (having children and intermarriage, rather than social reproduction—the processes through which a community perpetuates itself through time). Second, instead of considering actual practices in a manner that highlights innovation and change, scholars have indulged a primitivism that regards culture as if it were an inert heirloom handed down wholecloth from time immemorial. Third, rather than discuss racism as an array of ideological practices, studies have deployed a market model complete with an opportunity structure and a individual who voluntarily chooses among viable alternatives. For the sake of argument, let us call the three vices informing such studies biologism, primitivism, and voluntarism. I propose replacing them, respectively, with a broader sense of agency, the analysis of cultural practices, and the study of racism.

Although my project is theoretical, I hope to lend substance to abstractions by developing a positive critique of three studies on assimilation. The first study I find elegant, but fundmentally misleading. The other two studies I admire, and for the most part agree with. Precisely because we agree on so much, I feel that focused debate can be productive. In this respect my essay follows the venerable academic ritual of praising through critical analysis and disagreement. The topic of assimilation, if it is to be rethought, requires precisely this kind of pointed debate.

Let me begin with an essay by Douglas Massey (1981) entitled "Dimensions of the New Immigration to the United States and the Prospects for Assimilation." One immediately detects the article's note of fear (a conservative stance by a majority person, as outlined above): immigration during the 1970s has been of enormous proportions, approaching the high water mark for the twentieth century. Could the 1980s bring the feared flood? His central question is: can the United States assimilate these massive numbers of new immigrants? Massey speaks as if the nation were an organism attempting to absorb an unpalatable element newly entered in its environment.

Massey's biologism becomes most evident in the dubious assertion that, "Once intermarriage occurs, all other types of assimilation are held to follow automatically (Massey 1981: 70)." Why? After all, in the United States the children of intermarriage are often regarded as members of the ethnic group of one parent or the other, but not of both. Perhaps the dynamics emerge most clearly in black-Anglo intermarriages where the children, because of racism, are culturally viewed as black, not white (unless they "pass") and not a half-and-half genetic amalgam.

Massey's analysis considers the following factors: familism, fertility, intermarriage, residential segregation, political participation, and social mobility. Yet, in fact, all seven factors can be reduced to social mobility, the single variable of which they are functions. Massey puts the matter in the following terms:

> It should now be apparent that a key factor affecting the future of new immigrant groups in US society is social mobility. By whatever criteria considered—familism, fertility, political participation, residential segregation, or intermarriage—degree of social integration tends to increase with social class. The process of immigrant assimilation is fundamentally one of social mobility (1981: 72).

That is, the greater the degree of social mobility the smaller the family networks (familism), the fewer children born to women of suitable age (fertility), the higher the rates of marriage across ethnic lines (intermarriage), the smaller the proportion of people residing in barrios or ghettos (residential segregation), and the more people voting (political participation). The last item appears hopeful, but the good news of increased political participation goes hand-in-hand with the bad news of decreased participation in Chicano organizations.

What exactly do these findings represent? The social reproduction of cultural traditions, always a process that is selective and innovative as well as preservative, has been reduced to class affiliation where to be ethnic is to be working class. The reader is supposed to believe (despite, for example, the black bouregoisie) that to become middle class is to lose ethnic identity. Evidently, the process of assimilation involves approximations toward a putative Anglo (middle class) norm of isolated nuclear families with relatively few children. Rather than investigating the social consequences of "intermarriage," Massey assumes that the off-spring of such unions gravitate toward the cultural practices of the Anglo parent. His biologism may pressupose that intermarriage dilutes the race (despite the absence, culturally speaking, of half-blacks in the United States). Only his variable of residential segregation suggests that a cultural heritage is acquired through participation in community life.

Telling questions about assimilation should focus on community organization and the active processes of cultural selection and innovation. What constitutes the culture, and through what forms of life does it thrive, change, or languish? Instead of social reproduction and cultural creativity, Massay unfortunately offers biologism and social mobility as automatic producers of structural and cultural assimilation.

The second study I shall consider is comprised of a series of early articles by Miriam Wells (1975, 1976, 1980), an anthropologist who teaches at the University of California, Davis. Her admirable articles discuss assimilation in a small Wisconsin town (which she calls Riverside). She develops a model that depicts the interplay of the objective opportunity structure and subjective motivations. Wells describes her analysis in the following manner:

> The structural conditions outlined in the previous sections encouraged relocation but did not compel it. Understanding of the reasons why some chose to settle in Wisconsin and others continued to migrate is furthered by examination of the decision making process itself, the manner in which individuals and families weighed the costs and benefits of moving north (1976: 279).

The notion is that any society makes available certain opportunities, and not others, so that personal motivations dictate choices made among the socially available options. The underlying assumptions resemble those of neo-classical economists studying how people choose jobs or select commodities in a supermarket.

To simplify a more complex argument, Wells says that migrants passing through Riverside can decide either to remain in the migrant stream or to settle out by remaining in Wisconsin. Those who remain in the migrant stream usually have relatively strong personal networks of kinship, *compadrazgo*, and mutual indebtedness; those who settle out have relatively more ability in English, more education, and more varied occupational backgrounds than the former. The latter group, it would seem, is more assimilated than the former, yet the differences do not appear all that great (for example, 6.9 versus 5.8 median school years completed). Although Mexican migrants are not homogeneous, the differences between the two groups appear to be more a continuum than two polar types: the assimilated and the unassimilated.

When the Anglo population of Riverside is considered, the issue grows more complex. Although the town, in certain formal contexts, proclaims its cultural homogeneity, its informal practices point to hierarchically ordered divisions based on the following different national origins: Yankee elite (5%), Irish Catholic (10%), German Lutheran and Catholic (15%), and Polish (70%). These groupings correspond roughly with the historical sequence in which they migrated to Riverside as well as internal class lines. The informal practices through which these divisions are known and made real have to do with patterns of socializing. The elite enjoys its own literary and bridge clubs. The middle class has its Jaycees and Junior Women's Clubs. The working class plays at its bowling and snowmobile clubs. Even among so-called Anglos, assimilation has not produced a homogeneous group, as Wells explains in the following:

> The paradigm of assimilation does not adequately characterize the process or outcomes of intergroup relations in this case. Length of residence and exposure to a dominant culture do not compel a steady and unilinear homogenization (1975: 321).

Suppose Mexican migrants do settle out. How can they simply become Anglo when that population is itself so internally differentiated? Could not the conceptual difficulties in applying the paradigm of assimilation to the Anglo population similarly work against its application to the Mexican population?

A further factor prevents Mexican migrants from assimilating (assuming they wish to, which they may not). In ways that distinguish them from the Yankee, Irish, German, and Polish migrants of earlier periods, Mexicans confront a racist ideology that distinguishes them sharply from their predecessors to the small Wisconsin town. Wells describe this ideology, but she depicts it in terms of negative stereotypes rather than racism. Much as Sigmund Freud insisted on speaking about sexual rather than erotic attachments, analysts should not replace the term racism with more diluted euphemisms, such as stereotyping. Wells suggests that the negative stereotypes derive from experience with early migrants in the 1940s and "similar stereotypes held elsewhere in the United States (1980: 284)." Her depiction of the stereotypes works through a series of polar contrasts where the Anglos are stable, responsible, industrious, smart, clean, moral, optimistic, and the Mexicans are itinerant, irresponsible, lazy, stupid, dirty, criminal, fatalistic. Surely this list of opposed characteristics has been sufficiently publicized in the work of Octavio Romano and elsewhere, so that its existence can be attributed primarily to a pervasive pattern of American racism, and not to local experiences with Mexican migrants in the 1940s.

Racism, of course, involves practices as well as beliefs, and Wells develops a series of anecdotes about how matters work in everyday life. She tells, for example, of the Mexican who needs a leaky faucet repaired. Even after five phone calls, however, the Anglo plumber takes three weeks to arrive and do the job. Similarly, the Anglo city welfare director denies Mexican families emergency aid even though they meet the criteria of need and length of local residence. Informal practices thus work hand-in-hand with explicit prejudice in creating the pervasive humiliations that both reflect and create the notion that Mexican migrants are an inferior race. The interplay of opportunity structures and individual motivations in Wells's analysis fails to provide the terms for showing how apparent opportunities often cannot become real in practice for Mexican migrants. Wells's own analysis of racism (under the euphemistic name of stereotypes) highlights both the insights and the limits offered by her market model of voluntarism.

A third essay, this time by Jose Limon, will round out the discussion. Limon's elegant essay, entitled "Language, Mexican Immigration, and the 'Human Connection': A Perspective from the Ethnography of Communication," develops a micro-ethnography of El Redondo, a restaurant owned by middle class Mexican Americans that caters to Anglo Americans, and employs both Mexican Americans and undocumented Mexicans. His analysis shows that, just as the Anglo population of Riverside, Wisconsin, is internally differentiated, so too is the Mexican population in Austin, Texas. In order to depict this variation, Limon sets his characters in their distinctive scenes. Sitting at the tables are middle class Anglos. In the kitchen are the undocumented Mexican workers, two cooks and a dish handler. Standing before a long horizontal window are two Mexican American waitresses shouting their customers' orders to the cooks. At the edge of the dining floor by their carts are the busboys, undocumented Mexican workers whose life chances differ markedly from those of the cooks. Although the cooks make higher wages, the busboys interact more with the Mexican-American waitresses and thereby more rapidly learn English, enter an indefinite period of bilingualism, and enhance their long-run chances of job improvement. So far, so good.

The analysis considers yet another scene, the after hours bar scene, where what

Victor Turner would have called a liminal space is cleared. Limon sketches the scene in these terms:

> [L]ate at night, between ten and midnight, after the restaurant has closed, a mild symbolic inversion occurs in the bar. During this time the owner permits all of his workers to sit around the bar and have drinks for half price. Mexican American waitresses, undocumented Mexicans, the owner and his family and a few privileged Anglo and Mexican American middle-class regulars sit around with a mild and temporary suspension of role/status differences, engaged in free-flowing conversations ranging from the Mexican oil economy to the fate of football teams (pp. 202–203).

The owners permit a liminal space within which people who earlier inhabited the mini-scenes—sitting at tables, in the kitchen, before the long window, at the edge of the dining floor—become part of a larger conversation. The owners have enabled the temporary and partial suspension of class and ethnic differences.

The restaurant owners appear to be middle class, Republican, and barely fluent in Spanish. Yet they hang out in the after hours bar, and during the daylight hours their restaurant is a complex scene of cultural reproduction, conflict, and change. In certain respects, the restaurant as a cultural scene works against the conservatism of the owners who appear as agents of social reproduction without fully intending to do so. El Redondo restaurant does not simply maintain static culture form, but it produces creative ferment, a complex mix of innovation and preservation.

Limon's insightful sociolinguistic analysis provides the kind of circumstancial case material needed to study the complexity of assimilation processes. In general, processes of social reproduction and cultural perpetuation need not reflect the views of their agents. People's actions can have consequences they do not imagine, foresee, or intend. In the case Limon presents, the conservative restaurant owners have largely unwittingly created a complex scene of cultural vitality.

Cultures are always in process, borrowing and lending across their porous boundaries, and inventing ever new scenes and combinations of scenes. Had the Mexicans working in El Redondo restaurant stayed in Mexico, they could well be subjected to conditions leading to other changes and creative transformations in their ways of life. The notion of cultural reproduction thus should not be reduced, as it was in Massey's analysis, to biological reproduction. Nor should it imply that things must stay as they were, preserving an authentic relic, the true primitive culture, just as it was. Indeed, even if the owners lost their Spanish entirely, they still would be key agents in an institution that perpetuates a changing culture through time.

To recapitulate, my argument has been that assimilation studies have three key terms that need replacement. These terms are biologism, primitivism, and voluntarism.

Voluntarism suggests that assimilation involves formally free choices within a socially given opportunity structure. The notion is that society presents its members with a specific set of options. Its members, in turn, choose among those options based on their personal motivations. This was the analysis in Wells (1976).

Yet other writings by Wells highlight the import of racist ideology, both as formal beliefs and as informal practices. The choices people make may be more apparent than real when one takes into account the small brutalities of everyday life that Mexican migrants can encounter when they try to have leaky faucets repaired. The analysis of racism should displace voluntarism.

48

Primitivism suggests that assimilation is the movement from an authentic culture that is regarded as if it were a relic to be preserved just as it was. Yet cultures, in all times and in all places, undergo ongoing processes of change. Even as one generation succeeds another, the successors select, innovate, and recombine elements from the culture of their predecessors. The process combines continuity and change, old patterns and new developments.

Indeed, both Wells and Limon point to the internal differentiations of both Anglo and Mexican cultures, for neither is homogeneous. This fact in itself makes the notion of a linear movement of assimilation from Mexican to Anglo problematic. The complication only deepens if one considers that assimilation need not be a hydraulic process where as one rises the other falls. People could become increasingly fluent in an Anglo cultural milieu at the same time that they become more fluent in a local Mexican culture. Whether the latter fluency involves Mexican standard Spanish, rural Mexican speech, or Chicano English depends on the ongoing practices of a local community.

Biologism suggests that the unit of reproduction is the biological individual who, of course, must have children in order to perpetuate herself through time. To suggest that people, as they become middle class, follow middle class norms of family size and occupation conflates class and culture. Such people, after all, may be, not assimilated, but simply middle class. Under certain circumstances, perhaps, securely middle class people could be more assertive about their ethnicity than those in transition between classes.

The key questions of cultural reproduction involve the means by which communities, movements, and institutions perpetuate themselves through time, as dynamic changing constellations and not as static entities. El Redondo restaurant provides a context within which dynamic cultural reproduction takes place. No matter how much they stutter and no matter how they vote, the conservative relatively assimilated middle class owners are at the same time key agents in this process of cultural reproduction. My analysis simply suggests that a person's individual degree of assimilation should not be automatically confused with their role in the larger process of cultural reproduction.

REFERENCES

Dohrenwend, Burce P. and Robert J. Smith. 1962. "Toward a Theory of Acculturation." *Southwest Journal of Anthropology* 18: 30–39.

Gordon, Milton M. 1964. *Assimilation in American Life: The Role of Race, Religion, and National Origins.* New York: Oxford University Press.

Limon, Jose. 1986. "Language, Mexican Immigration, and the 'Human Connection': A Perspective from the Ethnography of Communication." In *Mexican Immigrants and Mexican Americans: An Evolving Relation,* eds. Harley L. Browning and Rodolfo O. de la Garza. Austin: The University of Texas Press, Center for Mexican American Studies. pp. 194–210.

Massey, Douglas. 1981. "Dimensions of the New Immigration to the United States and the Prospects for Assimilation." *American Review of Sociology* 7: 57–85.

Wells, Miriam. 1975. "Ethnicity, Social Stigma, and Resource Mobilization in Rural America: Reexamination of a Midwestern Experience." *Ethnohistory* 22 (4): 319–343.

Wells, Miriam. 1976. "Emigrants from the Migrant Stream: Environment and Incentives in Relocation." *Aztlan* 7(2): 267–290.

Wells, Miriam. 1980. "Oldtimers and Newcomers: The Role of Context in Mexican American Assimilation." *Aztlan* 11(2): 271–295.

EN TORNO A LA "TEORIA DE LAS DOS CULTURAS" Y SU APLICACION A LA LITERATURA CHICANA.

Lauro Flores

ABSTRACT

Este trabajo constituye una respuesta polémica a los planteamientos teóricos expuestos por Dieter Herms en su artículo "La literatura chicana y la teoría de las dos culturas." Aquilatando primero el carácter general y los aspectos acertados de la propuesta de Herms, la segunda parte de esta discusión examina en detalle varios puntos problemáticos contenidos en la misma. Teniendo fundamentalmente en cuenta las implicancias ideológicas que tales puntos conllevan, los problemas específicos que aquí se debaten son de orden teórico, metodológico y de exposición.

Uno de los problemas quizás más graves que han aquejado a la literatura chicana, a la cultura chicana en general, ha sido la poca atención que ha merecido por parte de la crítica "establecida" o "aceptada." Hasta hace muy poco, y con contadas excepciones, los productos culturales chicanos han sido comentados casi exclusivamente por críticos chicanos. Este hecho no tendría nada de particular de no conducir a una especie de *ghettoización* que, si nada más, ahonda el aislamiento de la cultura chicana y retarda consecuentemente el entendimiento entre los chicanos y otros grupos humanos.

Por tanto, resulta siempre grato que un autor no chicano, como el profesor alemán Dieter Herms, se tome la molestia de dedicar un artículo de seis páginas con treinta notas al problema de la interpretación de la cultura chicana, especialmente cuando tal trabajo aparece en una publicación con la importancia y el alcance de distribución de que goza la revista mexicana *Plural*.[1] La satisfacción es doble cuando la discusión, repleta de buenas intenciones, se emite, como lo hace el profesor Herms, desde una postura no sólo amigable sino que intenta además defender y legitimar la validez de la cultura chicana poniendo en tela de juicio las nociones de "anticultura" y "subcultura" que a veces se utilizan para calificarla.

Sin embargo, y con ello se cumple aquello de que las buenas intenciones a veces no bastan, una lectura atenta del ensayo de Herms revela rápidamente que el autor incurre en varios errores a lo largo de su exposición—algunos, en mi opinión, bastante serios. La discusión de los puntos cuestionables que Herms incluye en sus observaciones constituye, pues, el principal motivo de estas notas. No hay en ellas ninguna pretensión de ser exhaustivas; el espíritu en el que se escriben es de diálogo y la intención principal es contribuir a aclarar la comprensión de una realidad por demás compleja.

Herms plantea como proyecto general la posibilidad de rescatar ciertas partes de la tesis de V. I. Lenin sobre las dos culturas y utilizarlas en la explicación de algunos problemas actuales. Lo que propone el autor, específicamente, es manejar tales postulados como herramiento teórica que permita realizar un análisis acertado de la cultura chicana, de las obras literarias chicanas en particular.

Para tal efecto, Herms dispone su argumentación en tres partes principales. Sienta primero, muy rápidamente, las bases de lo que él entiende (erróneamente, según veremos) como "la teoría de las dos culturas" de Lenin y explica por qué la tesis es válida aún en nuestros días, especialmente en el caso de los EE.UU. Hace después un breve repaso del proceso de desarrollo bajo una dominación colonial que ha caracterizado la historia del pueblo chicano, con algunas de las consecuencias que de ello se desprenden (por ejemplo la continuidad de imágenes culturales que porta la potencia dominante vs. la discontinuidad de imágenes de rebelión y resistencia del grupo dominado), el papel que la literatura ocupa dentro de la producción ideológica en la superestructura de una sociedad dada, y la función y límites de la crítica literaria en tal proceso. Pasa sequidamente Herms a describir en qué consiste la aplicación de su enfoque de las dos culturas al análisis de textos literarios chicanos, subrayando aquellos problemas en los que se interesa particularmente el método, y haciendo de paso un veloz recuento de temas, motivos y recursos narrativos en diversas obras chicanas, especialmente en aquéllas que a su parecer (o al parecer de otros críticos en este campo) son las más importantes. Da, en su conclusión, algunos consejos y termina diciendo que la literatura chicana es, en su mayor parte, una literatura de la paz y por consiguiente forma parte de la lucha por "sobrevivir y crear condiciones de vida decentes y dignas en una democracia que funcione como tal."

Muy difícil sería rechazar en conjunto una visión que, en general, se antoja justa y equilibrada de lo que ha sido y es la literatura chicana. Los problemas que se traslucen en la discusión de Herms y que aquí nos conciernen son más específicos: algunos teóricos, otros ideológicos, y los demás, al parecer, de exposición. Para facilitar la presente discusión, procederemos aquí siguiendo someramente el orden de las secciones en que queda distribuido el trabajo del propio Herms.

La teoría: fuentes, realidades y aplicaciones.

Independientemente del manejo suelto, no bien delineado, del término *cultura* (y de algunos otros, como *nación*),[2] el principal problema de fondo que salta de inmediato a la vista en el artículo de Herms reside en su peculiar interpretación—y aplicación a la realidad cultural y política de EE.UU., según veremos más adelante—del concepto central de las "dos culturas" que él dice extraer o derivar de los escritos de Lenin.

Herms arguye acertadamente que, puesto que la estructura fundamental del sistema capitalista sigue siendo hoy esencialmente la misma que existía en las sociedades capitalistas clásicas de Europa a comienzos de siglo (aquéllas a las que Lenin—según Herms—tenía en cuenta al hacer sus observaciones al respecto), resulta válido trasladar algunas partes de la tesis leniniana al presente (p. 34). Hasta aquí, ningún problema.[3]

Pasa a afirmar el autor en segundo término, con profunda razón, que puesto que Lenin se dirigía en la Rusia presocialista a un conglomerado multinacional, su teoría adquiere un mayor grado de relevancia en nuestros días ''si se la aplica a una *cultura nacional* en resistencia, a un movimiento de *liberación cultural nacional* contra el colonialismo y el neocolonialismo'' (p. 34, énfasis mío). Con todo esto—y sin entrar por el momento en las implicancias que conlleva lo de ''liberación cultural nacional''[4]—uno supondría que Herms se ha estado encaminando específicamente hacia el análisis de una posible dicotomía *dentro de la cultura chicana,* sobre lo cual volveremos más adelante. Sin embargo, el autor pasa a postular en seguida una curiosa noción de *dos* culturas en los Estados Unidos basándose exclusivamente en su observación de que ''El debate reciente sobre la etnicidad *(ethnicity)* en las ciencias sociales norteamericanas ha comprobado con razón [?], un enfrentamiento o una colisión de *dos culturas,* en EE.UU., a saber: las culturas negra, americana nativa, chicana, puertorriqueña, etcétera [?], contra la cultura blanca, angloamericana; la subordinada contra la dominante, la minoría contra la corriente principal'' (p. 35, énfasis original de Hermes).

Los problemas que de aquí se desprenden son evidentes. Por un lado, o leemos mal o Herms alude no a dos sino a *varias* culturas; aun más, a varios problemas con particularidades históricas y culturales y ramificaciones políticas bastante diversas.[5] No se trata de negar que las llamadas ''minorías étnicas'' de los EE.UU. compartan históricamente muchas experiencias y características similares: la discriminación, la segregación, la opresión y la explotación económica, entre otras y *en general,* aunque esto también hay que matizarlo.[6] Pero con esto hay que tener cuidado, de otra manera se está en peligro de caer en la postura clásicamente chauvinista que adoptan algunos sociólogos y los organismos oficiales en los EE.UU., y que consiste en ''amontonar'' a todos los grupos de minorías, como quien mezcla nabos y coles. Tal actitud llevada al extremo se destila con grotesca exactitud en la expresión racista: ''they are all the same'' (''todos son iguales'').

Ahora bien, al escribir sus ''Observaciones críticas sobre la cuestión nacional''[7] (el texto en que el autor apoya su tesis) Lenin se dirigía, según señala el mismo Herms, a una audiencia multinacional. No sólo esto, sino que al recoger el tema respondía coyunturalmente a una necesidad política del momento (''Es obvio que la cuestión nacional se ha hecho prominente entre los problemas de la vida pública en Rusia,'' dice Lenin en la primera línea de su artículo) y más específicamente aún a una necesidad organizativa del Partido Social-Demócrata ruso. A la efervescencia de un nacionalismo acentuado entre los grandes rusos (el grupo dominante o mayoritario) se sumaba una ola de ''vacilaciones nacionalistas entre los social-demócratas 'nacionales' (i.e., no rusos) que—escribe Lenin—han llegado al extremo de violar el Programa del Partido.''[8] Así, la frase que abre el segundo párrafo de las ''Observaciones'' aclara contundentemente tanto la intención del autor como el público al que se dirigía: ''Este artículo persigue un objetivo especial, el de examinar en su aspecto general, precisamente aquellas vacilaciones de programa en que incurren marxistas y supuestos marxistas sobre la cuestión nacional.''[9]

Al avanzar su ''teoría de las dos culturas,'' Lenin no hablaba pues de una sociedad (multinacional) rusa dividida en una cultura rusa blanca, por un lado, y otra compuesta de todas las minorías nacionales juntas. Lo que señalaba, concretamente, era que todas y cada una de tales culturas (la rusa, la georgiana, la ucrania, etc.) encarnaban en realidad dos culturas: la cultura de la ''masa de trabajadores explotados" por un lado, y la cultura de "las clases acomodadas" por el otro.

Es claro que, al hacer sus aseveraciones, Herms no entraña una intención deliberadamente chauvinista sino que quiere destacar lo que existe de común entre las varias minorías que habitan en los EE.UU. Sin embargo, de ser así, y parece necio repetir lo obvio, también hay aspectos de "la cultura blanca, angloamericana," de una segunda cultura "blanca," hay que precisar—los propios proletarios y demás segmentos no burgueses que forman parte y son portadores de tal cultura, por ejemplo—, que comparten muchos rasgos con sus contrapartes "étnicas," y que se deben reconocer como tal.

Plantear pues una dicotomía absoluta entre cultura "blanca" y cultura(s) no-blanca(s) y hacer caso omiso de consideraciones de clase es un error. Lenin, en la mismas "Observaciones," dice que "En cualquier asunto político realmente serio y profundo se toma partido según la clase, no según la nación."[10] A esto se le puedo añadir, sin temor a equivocarse, no según el color de la piel o de la cultura. Si metodológicamente Herms propone que los textos literarios se deben leer a la luz del trasfondo histórico en el que se producen y teniendo siempre en cuenta los circuitos de recepción y distribución que les corresponden, ello es quizás más imprescindible en el caso de un texto expresamente político como las notas de Lenin.

Lectura y reconstrucción social del texto.

De todo lo anterior se puede deducir que una aplicación adecuada de las ideas de Lenin identificaría en la literatura chicana la expresión no de una cultura chicana (en sí misma o fundida con las otras "culturas étnicas" de este país), sino de dos. Una que se subscribe y sustenta en mayor o menor grado la ideología de las clases dominantes (las cuales no son sólo "blancas") y otra que presenta predominantemente elementos de una cultura de resistencia y protesta social.

Queda por entendido que todo texto literario, en cuanto se produce dentro de un sistema social determinado y forma parte de la superestructura subjetiva de dicho sistema, conlleva una tendencia o una carga ideológica (en el sentido "suave" o general del término). La tendencia ideológica de cada obra, claro está, no tiene que manifestarse necesariamente en forma explícita. De hecho, en la mayoría de los casos los postulados ideológicos sólo quedan sugeridos o se implican sutil e inconscientemente en los diferentes elementos textuales o en la interrelación de estos. Por otra parte, es evidente que la dinámica textual puede incluir aspectos de ambas culturas (dominante y dominada, proletaria y de élite, reaccionaria y revolucionaria, etc.) en una misma obra y, por consiguiente, una aproximación dialéctica es indispensable para desentrañar cabalmente la ideología que, en un último análisis, predomina en un caso determinado.

En este sentido, la aproximación que propone Herms como "la reconstrucción social del texto, discutiéndolo de cara a su trasfondo histórico y poniendo las circunstancias de su producción en un contexto de distribución y recepción" (p. 36), no añade mucho a la metodología propuesta antes por Joseph Sommers.[11] El mismo admite esto al decir que "el enfoque de las dos culturas no llega a resultados drásticamente diferentes a los de la crítica chicana, realizada hasta la fecha" (p. 38).

De hecho, hablando en estricto rigor, este método parece quedarse corto pues pone de relieve casi unilateralmente los aspectos "humanistas," "antiimperialistas," "socialistas," etc., de los textos y tiende a opacar esa dialéctica intratextual que señalábamos antes (la existencia en un texto dado de elementos contradictorios, de "primera" y "segunda" cultura). Una aproximación de este tipo se antoja pues sustancialmente acrítica en cuanto destaca selectivamente como "positivos" algunos aspectos de las obras y tiende a ignorar lo demás. ¿Hasta qué punto se puede sostener, por ejemplo, que la "recuperación" de un pasado precolombino idealizado y mistificado opera en función de una ideología revolucionaria o progresista? ¿Cómo se puede interpretar positivamente una visión fatalista o estática del tiempo y de la historia, la cual se complementa a veces con una estructura narrativa cíclica o circular? Todo esto, aunque no totalmente divorciado, es independiente del resultado "estético" del texto y si se pone de relieve aquí es porque Herms dice que su enfoque "como método aplicado a la literatura está interesado en la calidad ideológica de un texto" (p. 36).

Es interesante notar que las obras que Herms selecciona como las mejores, como "obras maestras casi modernas clásicas" (p. 37), son todas de la primera etapa de desarrollo de la literatura chicana contemporánea durante la década de los 70's, momento que corresponde al clímax del movimiento político chicano: . . . *y no se lo tragó la tierra* (1971), *Floricanto en Aztlán* (1971)[12] y *La carpa de los rascuachis* (1972). Todas, además, fueron producidas por autores comprometidos en cierta medida en la "causa chicana," en el movimiento político-social de aquellos años (Tomás Rivera, Alurista, Luis Valdez y el Teatro Campesino, respectivamente), y cuya evolución ideológica y profesional ha seguido trayectorias distintas.

Mucho tiempo has transcurrido desde aquel entonces. La literatura y la crítica literaria chicanas han seguido su curso de desarrollo y un aparte de aguas se ha venido haciendo cada vez más patente. Por un lado, siguiendo o coincidiendo quizás con las pautas metodológicas establecidas por Sommers y otros, un grupo de críticos toma partido por un análisis literario con orientación socio-histórica y, por otro, una escuela de jóvenes literatos y académicos se empeñan en "universalizar" la literatura y crítica chicanas adoptando y adaptando modelos occidentales (europeos y estadounidenses) a sus formas de hacer y de criticar literatura.[13] En el campo de la crítica, los trabajos de Juan Bruce-Novoa,[14] entre otros y por ejemplo, serían prototipo de esta última tendencia, según lo han comentado ya polémicamente el mismo Joseph Sommers, Sylvia Lizárraga y otros.[15]

En su artículo, "From the Critical Premise to the Product," Sommers, después de fustigar el coqueteo de algunos críticos con el estructuralismo, la semiótica y la estilística como patrones preconcebidos con los que quieren revelar "la complejidad y la coherencia formal" en los textos chicanos, dice también que "Otros críticos como Juan Bruce-Novoa retienen la insistencia formalista de separar al texto de su realidad histórica o de su contexto social, pero no obstante quieren ir más allá de la forma al área del 'significado.' Esta aproximación al 'significado,' limitándolo al ámbito de lo imaginario, postula el texto como ubicado en un 'espacio imaginario,' como la experiencia creada, mental, que por sí sola puede proveer una alternativa a la experiencia vivida, el caos, a la injusticia y a la inmoralidad del mundo real."[16]

Dadas las obvias implicaciones que todo esto contiene, resulta un poco extraño pues que Herms afirme—refiriéndose a Sommers y Novoa—que su enfoque "hasta podría ser apropiado para salvar el antagonismo *aparente* (énfasis mío) entre estas dos posiciones" (p. 35).

Si en alguna forma se puede aplicar "la teoría de las dos culturas" es precisamente en la explicación de la divergencia de trayectorias que se ha venido dando en la actividad literaria chicana, divergencia que se acentúa cada vez más y que ilustra el proceso dialéctico de polarización que sufre la cultura chicana: dos distintas e irreconciliables concepciones del mundo.

Es verdad que Herms, al proponer su teoría, dice que "el enfoque también se interesa por la calidad estética de un texto, más exactamente: por la dialéctica textual de forma y contenido." Sin embargo, al hacer sus breves comentarios sobre cada una de las obras que enumera, tal proposición no queda claramente de manifiesto. Se podría decir, por supuesto, que no hay lugar en seis páginas para hacerlo, pero ni siquiera se acerca a ello. Al hablar por ejemplo de *Zoot-Suit* de Luis Valdez, la crítica de Herms se centra sobre "un incidente algo cínico" que tiene que ver con la publicidad y la promoción de la obra (el circuito de distribución). Su contenido, sumamente problemático según lo han señalado ya algunos críticos, queda totalmente al margen.[17]

Lo mismo sucede con los comentarios de Herms acerca de *Bless Me, Ultima,* los cuales constituyen más bien una apología que una aproximación crítica dialéctica. Es cierto que, refiriéndose al ciclo que constituyen las tres novelas de Rudolfo Anaya[18] (aunque no queda claro como se inserta *Ceremony of Brotherhood* en esa sección), Herms critica la ideología que se proyecta en la epifanía del paisaje—parte fundamental en los escritos del narrador—, la cual, se nos dice, "a veces tiende a degenerarse a un misticismo de sangre y tierra" (p. 39). En cambio, la única observación tímidamente controversial que encontramos respecto a la primera novela de este autor se centra, nuevamente, en torno a su circuito de recepción: "También podría haber algún problema con la lectura de *Bless Me, Ultima*—dice Herms—en las aulas de clase americanas, donde parece que a veces se interpreta como ejemplo de cultura mexicana [?] inofensiva, escapista, exótica, folklórica, que aumenta los estereotipos en vez de corregirlos" (p. 39). Ni una palabra que cuestione directamente el misticismo temático de la obra; nada acerca de las implicaciones de su estructura cíclica regida por cuatro muertes y diez sueños premonitorios, etc.[19] En vez de esto, Herms resume el asunto liberal y conciliatoriamente con un comentario que habla por sí solo: "No obstante, permanece un elemento fuerte de humanismo en la prosa de Anaya, y yo no veo por qué éste no debería contar con el amor como una de las piedras angulares de las emociones" (p. 39). No es tarea de la crítica literaria, creo, juzgar si un autor debe o no echar mano del amor o de cualquier otro elemento para cumplir su meta narrativa. Se trata de sopesar los elementos que integran la obra, la interacción y condicionamiento que estos sostienen entre sí y en relación con su contexto, para determinar después tanto el resultado estético como su carga ideológica. Esto a un primer nivel. Los circuitos de distribución y recepción son parte de un segundo nivel de discusión conectado, obviamente, al contexto.

Exposición y conclusiones.

La brevedad del artículo de Herms, y la enorme cantidad de información que el autor intenta incorporar en él es quizás el mayor problema que encontramos en los que a su exposición respecta. No hay, por lo tanto, evidencia de una profundización significativa en ninguno de los ejemplos textuales que se introducen. De hecho, en la mayoría de los casos, Herms se limita a repetir observaciones y juicios previamente formulados por otros críticos. De allí, como señalábamos antes, que él mismo se vea obligado a admitir que su enfoque no logra resultados substancialmente diferentes de los que otros estudiosos de la literatura chicana han logrado hasta ahora.

Por otra parte, resultaría difícil, por no decir que artificial, separar algunos problemas de exposición del trasfondo ideológico que connotan—aun si en algunos casos éste asume matices sumamente sutiles. Par ilustrar, y sin querer volver ahora

56

sobre lo de cultura blanca vs. cultura étnica, consideremos por un momento dos observaciones que Herms hace al evaluar el carácter proletario de un par de obras distintas: primera, "Con razón *Plum Plum Pickers* de Barrio fue llamado el *Grapes of Wrath (Las viñas de la ira)* chicano" (p. 39), y segunda, "La obra *Bracero* de Eugene Nelson, aunque literatura chicanesca, puede ser llamada con razón *The Jungle* de los chicanos" (p. 39). A manera de comentario, sólo diré que este tipo de comparaciones benévolas son rememorativas de algo que dijera hace años el crítico cubano Roberto Fernández Retamar a propósito de la relación colonial que ha existido entre Europa (y EE.UU.) y América Latina por siglos y que, aun después de la independencia política formal de nuestros países, se prolonga en actitudes y complejos: "Su nombre [el de los caribes]—escribe Retamar—es perpetuado por el Mar Caribe (al que algunos llaman simpáticamente el Mediterráneo americano; algo así como si nosotros llamáramos al Mediterráneo el Caribe europeo)."[20]

Cerca ya del epílogo de su artículo, Herms incluye una curiosa recomendación que resulta bastante reveladora: "Parece ser aconsejable que la cultura chicana [?] controlara su propia infraestructura distribucional [. . .] De esta manera existiría un control sobre sus propios rituales, habría un lazo común entre la producción, la distribución y la recepción de su creatividad" (p. 39). Es decir, que si se puede hablar de la cultura chicana en bloque, sin distinciones de clase de ningún tipo, se puede también invocar un regreso utópico a la primera etapa del capitalismo (en tanto sea éste un capitalismo chicano y no imperialista), según la caracterizan la libre empresa y la "democracia económica." Aun de ser factible un retroceso en la tendencia natural del sistema hacia los monopolios y la concentración del capital, uno no puede dejar de sonreír y preguntarse qué o quién es esa entidad abstracta, "la cultura," capaz de competir con las grandes corporaciones y de ser no sólo propietaria sino distribuidora de sí misma. O quizás de lo que se trata es de ir todavía más atrás (puesto que el autor deja bien claro en la penúltima frase de su artículo que "para los que luchan en el mundo imperialista occidental, la tarea inmediata no puede ser el socialismo"), ya que al principio del trabajo Herms dice que "la *segunda* cultura refleja el colectivismo, la producción de uso, el mercado de intercambio, la comunidad democrática, la propiedad colectiva" (p. 35).

Por lo demás, la recomendación de Herms, si pretende proveernos con una idea o alternativa novedosa, resulta un tanto cándida. Muchas revistas y pequeñas editoriales "independientes" (Quinto Sol, Justa, Arte Público, Maize, Bilingual Press, etc.) han estado realizando el valiente esfuerzo desde el principio mismo del *chicanismo* en los años 60. Muchas de las publicaciones, desgraciadamente, han sufrido una existencia sumamente irregular, han subsistido por algunos años y después han desaparecido ante las presiones del mercado (*Maize* es, notablemente, el caso más reciente).

Todo esto es congruente con lo que a nuestro juicio es, si no una mala lectura de Lenin, al menos una aplicación errada de sus tesis a la realidad norteamericana y a la interpretación del complejo de elementos culturales de que se compone el corpus literario chicano en particular.

Mientras se hable del problema chicano en general, de su ubicación dentro de esa totalidad conflictiva que es el conglomerado multinacional de los EE.UU., es legítimo hablar de una cultura chicana. Pero cuando se trata de entender su desarrollo histórico y su funcionamiento específico, concreto, tenalmente si para nuestro aproximación utilizamos o pretendemos utilizar los postulados de Lenin, encontraremos que en la literatura chicana se nuclean no una sino dos visiones del mundo, dos culturas que se perciben como una sola.

NOTAS

1. Dieter Herms, "La literatura chicana y la teoría de las dos culturas," *Plural*, 158 (noviembre de 1984), 34–39. Los números de página que acompañan citas o referencias al trabajo son de esta publicación. Este artículo se ha vuelto a publicar en inglés, en *Innternational Studies in Honor of Tomás Rivera* (Houston: Arte Público Press, 1986) [*Revista Chicano-Riqueña*, 13:3–4 (1985)].

2. *Nación*, y la alusión al término queda implícita en la utilización de los conceptos "cultura nacional" y "liberación nacional," según lo entendemos, es una categoría histórica, a diferencia de *etnia*. No se trata simplemente de una discrepancia terminológica. De hecho, las soluciones políticas de un conflicto dado, cuando de la cuestión nacional se trata, dependen de la realidad concreta con que se brega. En el caso de Puerto Rico, una *nación* colonizada directamente por los EE.UU., por ejemplo, no existe ninguna duda de que la solución política es la autodeterminación, la soberanía de Puerto Rico como entidad independiente.

3. La única salvedad que se podría hacer al respecto tiene que ver con la frase "sociedades capitalistas clásicas de Europa." Creo que, al utilizarla, Herms tiene en mente el modelo de desarollo económico capitalista que se gestó en el occidente de Europa. Sin embargo, el desarrollo de las estructuras políticas y sociales, como se sabe, fue algo distinto entre Oriente y Occidente. La formación de estados nacionales (mononacionales) que imperó en el occidente—con la excepción de la Gran Bretaña que abarcó más de una nación en su constitución como estado—no se dio de igual manera en el sector oriental, en donde de hecho el estado multinacional (Rusia como prototipo) fue la regla general. Es lógico deducir, por lo tanto, que al hablar del problema nacional Lenin tenía en mente ambos fenómenos. De esto, sin embargo, tiene que estar consciente Herms como lo demuestra la frase con la que inicia el tercer párrafo de su artículo: "Lenin se dirigía en la Rusia presocialista a un conglomerado de gente principalmente multinacional."

4. Me refiero con esto a la enconada polémica que sostuvieron el mismo Lenin y otros líderes bolcheviques contra los proponentes de la llamada "autonomía cultural nacional." Véanse por ejemplo el apartado número cuatro de las "Observaciones críticas sobre la cuestión nacional" (21–27)—el trabajo en que Herms basa sus ideas—que Lenin dedica a este problema y que lleva tal frase entrecomillada como subtítulo ("Cultural-Nacional Autonomy"), y el trabajo de J. V. Stalin, "El marxismo y la cuestión nacional."

5. No creo necesario, ni cabe aquí tampoco, señalar en minucia las diferencias que existen entre los varios grupos. Por lo demás, lo que a Herms parece interesarle, más que las diferencias, son los puntos en común.

6. Dentro de los grupos minoritarios existe también una estratificación social. La cuestión de clases entre los chicanos ha sido tratada, entre otros, por Mario Barrera (a quien Herms hace referencia) en su libro *Race and Class in the Southwest* (Notre Dame: University of Notre Dame Press, 1979) y todavía más específicamente en su artículo "Chicano Class Structure," incluido en la antología *Chicano Studies: A Multidisciplinary Approach*, editada por García, Lomelí y Ortiz (New York: Teachers College Press, 1984), 40–55. Para un análisis concerniente al caso negro, véase por ejemplo el trabajo de Nelson Peery, *The Negro National and Colonial Question* (Chicago: Proletarian Publishers, 1973), en donde el autor delínea el desarrollo no sólo de una pequeña burguesía sino de una "burguesía nacional" y una "burguesía compradora" negras. En el caso de Puerto Rico este asunto es todavía más claro. ¿Cómo hablar por consiguiente de *una* cultura chicana, de una cultura negra, de "*la* cultura blanca angloamericana"?

7. Este artículo lo escribió Lenin entre octubre y diciembre de 1913. Se publicó originalmente, ese mismo año, en la revista *Prosveshcheniye*, Nos. 10, 11 y 12, y después ha quedado recogido en el tomo 19 de las *Obras Completas* del autor. La Editorial Progreso de Moscú lo publicó en ingles, junto con varios otros artículos sobre el mismo tema ("The Right of Nations to Self-Determination," "The Socialist Revolution and the

Right of Nations to Self-Determination (Theses)" y "The Discussion of Self-Determination Summed up"), en 1951. La quinta edición de este trabajo (1971), comunmente conocido con el título del primer artículo, *Critical Remarts on the National Question*, es la que yo utilizo aquí.

8. *Critical Remarts*, p. 7. La traducción de ésta y las demás citas es mía.
9. *Critical Remarts*, p. 7.
10. *Critical Remarts*, p. 24.
11. "From the Critical Premise to the Product: Critical Modes and their Application to a Chicano Literary Text," en *The New Scholar*, 5:2 (1977). Reimpreso en forma modificada y con el título de "Critical Approaches to Chicano Literature," en *Modern Chicano Writers, A Collection of Critical Essays*, eds. Joseph Sommers y Tomá Ybarra-Frausto (New Jersey: Prentice-Hall, 1979), 31–40.
12. En el texto de su artículo, Herms se refiere erróneamente a esta obra come *Floricanto de Aztlán*. Evidentemente se trata de un error tipográfico ya que en la nota bibliográfica el título aparece en forma correcta.
13. Esta tendencia "universalista" o "universalizante" se manifiesta bien entre el grupo de escritores que el crítico Juan Rodríguez ha bautizado con el nombre de "spick-and-span poets," entre los que sobresalen Gary Soto y Alberto Ríos. El primer número de *Imagine* (Summer 1984), publicación dirigida por Tino Villanueva, también parece apuntar en cierta medida hacia esta vertiente.
14. Juan Bruce-Novoa, *Chicano Poetry. A Response to Chaos* (Texas: University of Texas Press, 1982). En este libro quedan resumidas las ideas que el autor ha venido postulando en años anteriores: "The Space of Chicano Literature," *De Colores*, 1:4 (1975), 22–42; "El deslinde del espacio literario," *Aztlán*, 11:2 (1980), 323–36.
15. "From the Critical Premise to the Product," en *The New Scholar*, y "Observaciones acerca de la crítica literaria chicana," en *Revista Chicano-Riqueña*, 10:4 (Fall 1982), 55–64, respectivamente.
16. *The New Scholar*, 56.
17. Yvonne Yarbro-Bejarano y Tomás Ybarra-Frausto, " 'Zoot-Suit Mania' Sweeps L.A., Moves Toward East," *In These Times*, (Jan. 31–Feb. 6, 1979), 23. Para una crítica general del Teatro Campesino, véase también el trabajo de Yarbro-Bejarano, "From *acto* to *mito:* A Critical Appraisal of the Teatro Campesino," en *Modern Chicano Writers*, eds. Joseph Sommers y Tomás Ybarra-Frausto (New Jersey: Prentice Hall, 1979), 176–185.
18. *Bless Me, Ultima* (Berkeley: Quinto Sol, 1972), *Heart of Aztlán* (Berkeley: Justa, 1976), *Tortuga* (Berkeley: Justa, 1979).
19. Véase el trabajo de Vernon E. Lattin, "The 'Horror of Darkness': Meaning and Structure in Anaya's *Bless Me, Ultima*, en *Revista Chicano-Riqueña*, 6:2 (1978), 50–57.
20. *Calibán. Apuntes sobre la cultura de nuestra América* (México: Diógenes, 1971), 13.

ANTICLERICALISM IN
TWO CHICANO CLASSICS

Lawrence Benton

ABSTRACT

Anticlericalism is important in both *Pocho* by José Antonio Villareal and *Y no se lo tragó la tierra* by Tomás Rivera. The protagonist of *Pocho* rejects his parents' Mexican Catholicism because he considers it incompatible with the dogma of individualism. By contrast, Rivera's hero curses God because of His indifference to the poor, hence raising the issues of class conflict and social justice. Villareal replaces Catholic faith with individualist ideology; Rivera attacks religion because it pacifies La Raza, thereby rendering it easy prey for exploitation. Anticlericalism is thus used to achieve diametrically opposed ends.

Both *Pocho* by José Antonio Villarreal and *Y no se lo tragó la tierra* by Tomás Rivera contain obvious anti-church sentiments. But the implications of anticlericalism in the former, or so I shall argue, are wholly different from those of the latter. *Pocho,* written in English and published by Doubleday, appeared in 1959—before the Chicano social and cultural movement of the 1960's had begun. *Y no se lo tragó la tierra,* written in Spanish, came out in 1972, well after the movement was under way, and was published by Quinto Sol, a Chicano press. Given these historical considerations one would expect literary products of a markedly different nature, and such is the case.

Except for the first chapter, which gives an account of how his father Juan immigrated from revolutionary Mexico to the U.S., *Pocho* is primarily the story of Richard Rubio, a Chicano who grew up in the Santa Clara Valley of California during the 1930s and 40s. His family, though not middle class by some standards, still manages to buy a home and maintain a decent material standard of life.

Richard is a remarkably precocious child who at the age of nine is already engaging in metaphysical speculation. The novel's third person omniscient narrator mentions perhaps ironically, that because of his tender age "Things were too complex for him" (p. 32). As he ponders the question "who made the world?" and its stock answer "God made the world," he realizes he does not yet know who God is. Then he remembers that "one does not question God", and for one brief moment he is satisfied. But immediately he grows doubtful: "... if there was nothing at the beginning what was there? Just a bunch of empty sky? But if there was even just empty sky it was *something!* and the darkness! Was not the darkness something!" [p. 33]

This passage sets the tone of skepticism which becomes even more pronounced as the boy matures to manhood. When the parish priest tells him that to touch a girl is a mortal sin and that it is "even worst to touch your own sister" (p. 35), he immediately sees a problem with the implied premise that there can be degrees of mortal sin (since the concept of mortality implies an absolute). When he discusses the issue with his mother, she is outraged to learn he knows about sex.

Later, when he is alone in his darkened room trying to understand his mother's sudden, inexplicable wrath, he asks himself how a God who is good could have created darkness (and, by implication, evil). The dark frightens him just as his ignorance of the sexual mystery causes him anxiety. "Bad things," he concludes, "have something to do with being alive" (p. 37). The naive child in two sentences expresses the contradiction between spirit and matter and isolates what for him will be the main sentiment associated with religion: fear. And fear generates anger. As his mother suffers the severe pain of childbirth, she assures him the Virgin is watching over her. He wanted to "holler out against the Lord and the Virgin for making her suffer", but instead he "got scared and crossed himself because he had a bad thought" (p. 39). As he grows older, his skepticism becomes his main weapon against the terror of God's punishment. His belief in reason slowly erodes his belief in religion until finally he becomes a confirmed nonbeliever.

The meaning of Richard's atheism, as well as its genesis, can better be understood if one realizes the faith he rejects is much more than a mere set of intellectual precepts. It functions as the ideological foundation of his parents' way of life. This association of religion with ideology emerges clearly in a conversation between the boy and his mother. She expresses her hope that he will become a priest or, failing that, " 'go to the university . . . to learn how to make more money than you would make in the fields or the cannery. So you can change our way of living somewhat, and people could see what a good son we had and it would make us all something to respect. Then, when you married and began your family, you would have a nice home and could be assured that you would be able to afford an education for your children' " (p. 63). But Richard objects to this argument on the grounds that he considers his primary obligation not to others but to himself: "I do not care about making a lot of money and about what people think and about the family in the way you speak. I have to learn as much as I can so, so that I can live . . . learn for *me* for *myself*—ah, but I cannot explain it to you, and you would not understand me if I could" (p. 63).

"That kind of thinking is wrong," his mother replies, "and unnatural—to have that kind of feeling against the family and the custom. *It is as if you were speaking against the church.*" (emphasis added) He continues to defend his motives, warning her that he may not "find time to make a family, for the important thing is that I must learn" (p. 64). Then, even though he has nothing against the church, she calls him blasphemous, thus associating religion with tradition. This connection—and its corollary which equates nonbelief with rejection of custom, family and the Mexican way of life—is made manifest throughout the work.

In succeeding chapters Richard's anticlericalism grows in intensity. He accuses nuns and priests of lying and makes friends with an adult agnostic named Joe Pete Mañoel who, even though he refuses to discuss such issues as the Immaculate

Conception, nevertheless functions as a kind of cultural hero. The young boy respects him more than he does the priest who enjoins him to "just believe" (p. 85). Joe Pete, accused of impregnating a thirteen year old girl, goes mad and is committed to the state hospital for the insane. Richard believes he is innocent and is shocked by the realization that the community considers Joe Pete's agnosticism a more serious crime than his offense against the girl. In Richard's mind Joe Pete is a martyr to religious bigotry.

Meanwhile, the Rubio family is falling apart. Paternal authority, central to the cohesion of the Mexican family, has in this alien place come increasingly under attack. The women of the family—the mother as much as the sisters—more and more reject the father's jurisdiction over their lives. Gradually Richard comes to believe the real source of disharmony is the family's attempt to live according to customs which are incompatible with U.S. society. This insight comes to him in a poignant passage in which he is quarrelling with his mother about women's rights. She tells him the law protects her from being beaten by her husband. That his mother would approve of such a law dismays Richard. He asks her point blank: "Mamá, would you really have my father put in jail?" "Yes, I would," (p. 93), she replies. Suddenly he understands that his mother is also "locked up." He cries as he thinks of his future and that of his sisters: ". . . and starkly, without knowledge of the words that could describe it, he saw the demands of tradition, of culture, of the social structure on an individual. Not comprehending, he was again aware of the dark mysterious force, and was resolved that he would rise above it." In the darkness he suddenly sits up and says: "¡Mierda! ¡Es pura mierda!" He understands that he will never again be "wholly Mexican" (p. 95).

From this point on, Richard slowly accepts the North American way of life. He understands, though he cannot express in words, what his mother had implied: that the "dark mysterious force" of tradition arises out of the Catholic faith as believed in and practiced by his parents. In a process which stretches out over several years, he realizes that if he is to live fully as an "American" he must first rid himself of the values implied by this tradition. The moral and ethical system it entails cannot be reconciled with life in America as he understands it. Hence, though perhaps not always deliberately, for him impiety and acculturation go hand in hand.

By the time he reaches adolescence, Richard still believes in God but—in spite of clerical threats—no longer fears Him. Relations between him and the parish priest are rapidly deteriorating because of various "sins of the flesh" which he commits frequently and which he believes the prelate enjoys hearing him confess, particularly those which have to do with his fantasies about Sister Mary Joseph. After one such disclosure he refuses to take communion and walks defiantly out of the church.

This anticlerical behavior reaches its climax in an agonizingly painful argument between Richard and his father over the familiar issue of paternal authority. When informed he is not allowed out of the house after 9:00 p.m. he says: "But I must live my life." His father's angry reply rejects the implied premise of the cult of individualism: "Your life belongs to us even after you marry, because we gave it to you. You can never forget your responsibility to the family' " (p. 129). In the dispute which follows Richard insists on his right to live his *own* life. Juan Rubio insists that Richard is responsible not only to his family but to *La Raza* as well: "You have fulfilled but a part of your debt to your race," he says, "but you are young yet and must fulfill the destiny of your God. When you are older you will marry and have a family. Then you will know why you are here. That is God's will." (p. 131). Richard rejects this argument bluntly: "No, father . . . if that is all there is to it, if one must marry and have a family and live like this, only working to eat and feed the family, not really living or having anything to live for, then I will never marry . . . *There is something inside, father! Something I want and do not know."* (emphasis added) His father contends adamantly that "It is God's will that we live as we do." Richard says that in that case "There must be something wrong with God." This sacrilege reduces Juan Rubio to tears. He tries to explain to his son ". . . that one cannot fight the destiny. . . ." At this juncture, Richard asks the question which brings the argument to a close and which contains the genesis of the new ideology: "And are you happy, Father" (p. 131)? Juan says he is, but Richard considers his father miserably *un*happy—tied to a treadmill of manual labor and poverty made necessary by responsibilities to the family, the race—everybody except one's very own self, the private person who exists in his own right and primarily for his own sake.

In fact, it is just this concern for the rights and happiness of each member as an individual, separate entity which comes to characterize the Rubio family and which ultimately destroys it. The father's authority at last fails completely. All flatly refuse to obey him until, in one final attempt to regain his former status, he goes on a wild rampage, beating his wife and children and savagely "destroying everything he had built or accumulated with his own hands" (p. 167). Having done this, he abandons the family altogether and eventually asks for a divorce so that he can marry the young girl with whom he is living and who is expecting his child.

With the departure of his father, Richard temporarily assumes the role of "head" of the household. He repeatedly makes it clear, however, that he is first and foremost concerned with his own individual welfare as opposed to that of the family. So it is not surprising that when his mother praises him for complying with his "duty" to take care of her and his sisters rather than attend the university, he contradicts her: "It is not my duty, Mamá . . . I am doing what I am doing because I do not want to do anything else at the moment, but please do not mistake my motives" (p. 171). She doubts he can really feel this way and tells him the family should "all go together to the church" since they are starting a new life and ". . . it would be a good thing to receive a blessing from the Lord." She is stunned when he informs her that he has left the church and no longer believes in God. Of this announcement the narrator comments: "at last he was really free" (p. 172).

Having divested himself of the old ideology, he no longer need continue "living a lie." Since the first theological debate with his mother, he has stressed the importance of individualism. "What people thought was honorable was not important," the narrator says, referring to the adolescent Richard, "because he was the important guy. No matter what he did and who was affected by his actions, in the end it came back to himself and his feelings. He was himself, and everything else was there because he was *himself,* and it wouldn't be there if it were not for himself, and then of course it wouldn't matter to him" (p. 108). Later he thinks "Never—, no, never—will I allow myself to become part of a group—to become classified *to lose my individuality"* (p. 152). (emphasis added) When some Anglo liberals with whom he becomes friendly encourage him to dedicate his life to "the Mexican cause," he doubts there is such a thing; and he disagrees with "some of their ideas, because they constitute a threat to his individuality" (p. 175).

It is understandable then that his mother's appeals that he stay with the family fall on deaf ears. He has decided to leave, and though he promises to send her money his mother tells him he is wrong to desert the family. But he decides it is best "to run away from the insidious tragedy of such an existence" (he enlists in the military), even though he considers it wrong to use the war, "a thing he did not

63

believe in, to solve his problems" (p. 185). The novel ends as Richard is riding on a troop train "thinking little of the life he had left behind him—only of the future" (p. 186). For a moment he thinks about some of the people he had known and asks himself "what of them—and why? Of what worth was it all?" Then he asks what has become the most important question of all: "*What about me?* . . . and suddenly he knew that for him there would never be a coming back" (p. 187).

At last theory and praxis combine to form a cohesive whole: Richard's actions have come into accord with his beliefs. For some time now he has conceived of his interests as existing apart from and in opposition to those of others, including his family. He abandons it for what he concedes to be purely selfish motives. And yet, he is little more culpable of such indifference toward the common good than his sisters or even his mother, who insists so vehemently on her legal rights against her husband and who sounds "almost happy" (p. 171) as she contemplates her future life without him.

Unlike them, however, Richard understands with some degree of explicitness that the changes in the family's way of life imply a concomitant change of ideological sanction. His parents' Catholicism, with its emphasis on *la familia y la Raza,* seems unsuited to a life in which the family and ethnic group as such are less important than the individuals who comprise them. The U.S. legal system places great emphasis on the belief that fundamental rights should be conferred on individual persons as such, that all persons (at least in theory) are "equal" before the law. (In such a system the hegemony of the father—as Juan Rubio learned—is much more limited than it is in most Latin countries, certainly including Mexico; this fact alone, as the author implies several times, accounts at least to some extent for the demise of the family).

It is beyond the scope of this paper to analyze this dogma at length. What is to the point here is that whether it is a question of Lockean liberalism or the pragmatic utilitarianism of J. S. Mill and Dewey (perhaps the two most widely held political ideologies in U.S. life), there is no disagreement that "the authority of government resides in the individual's right to his or her own self preservation" (Bayes 63). Richard does not take this expression to mean the acquisition of property, as did Locke. He wants, rather, the right to "live my life" (p. 129), as he tells his father, to pursue the quest for what he calls that "something inside . . . something I want and do not know" (p. 131). He wants, in other words, to devote himself to the end defined and extolled by the founding fathers and all generations since: The pursuit of happiness, which of course means above all *his own* happiness as he himself defines it. The adoption of this doctrine in word and deed puts him in accord with the advice that he as a young boy had given his father: "This is America, father . . . if we are to live in this country we must live like Americans" (p. 133).[1]

Y no se lo tragó la tierra is decidedly less "American", at least in this sense, and certainly this is not the only difference.

It consists of twelve episodes all of which are structured loosely around the life of an anonymous Chicano boy whose parents are migrant workers in Texas. Introductory and closing chapters unify the intervening episodes, thereby establishing their thematic consistency. Most of the chapters are preceded by a brief anecdote. In contrast to *Pocho,* which is technically quite conventional, *Y no se lo tragó la tierra* makes use of many narrative techniques, chief among which are an extreme economy of expression (the work is little more extensive than a long short story); the use of interior monologues and a Greek-like chorus which represents the collective voice of the community. The characters, all of whom speak in the authentic idiom of popular language, have no individual identity and so emerge as archetypes. The collective and social are thus emphasized rather than the individual.

One of the anecdotes portrays an avaricious Spanish priest, and some of the episodes contain mild impiety.[2] "Primera comunion", for example, presents a humorous sketch of the boy protagonist's first communion, at which, just to be safe, he confesses to 200 sins, though he has committed only 150.

The most extreme anticlericalism, however, occurs in the chapter from which the title is taken and in which the boy curses God. The first part of this episode gives an account of the frustration the boy feels because his father has had a sunstroke and he can do nothing to help him. His father grows worse and the boy thinks he will die. He is angry as he hears his parents beg God for mercy. His mother lights candles, a practice which, as he points out, has not worked in previous emergencies. In a burst of revulsion he suddenly pours out his wrath at the injustice they all must suffer:

> ¿Por qué es que nosotros estamos aquí como enterrados en la tierra? O los microbios nos comen o el sol nos asolea. Siempre alguna enfermedad. Y todos los días, trabaje y trabaje. ¿Para qué? Pobre papá, él que le entra parejito. Yo creo que nació trabajando. Como dice él, apenas tenía los cinco años y ya andaba con su papá sembrando maíz. Tanto darle de comer a la tierra y al sol y luego, saz, un día cuando menos lo piensa cae asoleado. Y uno sin poder hacer nada. Y luego ellos rogándole a Dios . . . si Dios no se acuerda de uno . . . yo creo que ni hay . . . (p. 48)

Fearing his father will worsen, however, and wanting there to be something to give the poor man hope, he retreats from an outright denial of God's existence. When his mother reassures him that God will save his father he reminds her of the misfortunes of his uncle and aunt, whom God did not save from death and of their orphaned children. He concludes that "a Dios le importa poco a uno de los pobres." He demands to know why they have to live under such conditions: "Ya me canso de pensar, ¿por qué? ¿por qué usted? ¿Por qué papá? ¿por qué mi tío? ¿por qué mi tía? ¿por qué sus niños? ¿Dígame usted por qué? ¿Por qué nosotros nomás enterrardos en la tierra como animales sin ningunas esperanzas de nada?" She tells him: "Sólo la muerte nos trae el descanso a nosotros." His reply goes to the heart of the matter: "*¿Pero, por qué a nosotros?*" (p. 50). (emphasis added) The first section ends as he scoffs at her implied argument that the poor will go to heaven.

Part two of the episode, which takes place the following day, offers more evidence that the boy's arguments against God are well founded. Because his mother must remain at home to care for his father, he must take charge of his brothers and sisters as they work in the fields. The day dawns cloudy but by mid-morning the children are beginning to suffer from the heat and he warns them to be careful: "Ya vieron lo que le pasó a papá por andar aguantando. El sol se lo puede comer a uno" (p. 52). By three o'clock they are soaked with sweat and at four the youngest brother—who is only nine years old—begins to vomit and collapses into spasms. Filled with despair, the boy again recites the litany of rhetorical questions: "¿Por qué a papá y luego a mi hermanito? Apenas tiene los nueve años. ¿Por qué? Tiene que trabajar como un burro enterrado en la tierra. Papá, mamá, y éste mi hermanito, ¿qué culpa tienen de nada?" (p. 54)

As he carries his brother toward the house he grows angrier and begins to swear. He curses God. He is afraid the earth will swallow him up, but it is harder than ever, so he vents his anger by cursing God once more. Immediately after committing this blasphemy he notices his brother seems to have improved.

That night, no longer concerned about the sick, all that he anticipates is "la frescura de la mañana". By dawn both his father and brother have recuperated. As the episode draws to a close, the morning is cool and cloudy, "y por primera vez se sentía capaz de hacer cualquier cosa que él quisiera" (p. 54).

What is at issue here is not so much the Deity's existence—though for one fleeting moment it is questioned—as it is His nature and what that nature implies. God is not accused of indifference toward humanity in general throughout all of history. If this were true then some sort of existential explanation might be in order. A careful reading of this episode and the novel in general, however, show that such is not the case. What is contended about The Deity is that He is discriminatory. He does not care about *poor* people. He discriminates on the basis of social class. The poor literally kill themselves working or, if fortunate enough to survive, fall victim to illnesses and disasters brought on by economic exploitation. The boy's fury is caused by his parents' inability to understand a contradiction. They plead with the self same God who, through Divine neglect, is responsible for their situation in the first place. So long as they cling passively to such false hope they will continue to be exploited. The boy condemns not only God but, by implication, the relations of production which account for the grim conditions described throughout the work. It is significant that only after the curse do his father and brother improve. And the heat which—at least in the immediate sense—caused their suffering is broken.

Heat is closely associated with suffering and injustice in several of the episodes. One little boy, driven by the heat to drink water from a cattle tank, is shot and killed by the boss in an attempt to "scare" him. A frustrated lover kills himself by clutching an electrical transformer. Two children die when a kerosene stove explodes (the boss would not allow their parents to bring them to the field). Sixteen farm workers are burned alive as they are being transported to work.

Heat becomes a metaphor for hell. The boy explains his fear of the inferno: "Lo que sí me daba miedo era el infierno porque unos meses antes me había caído en un baño de brasas que usábamos como calentador en el cuartito donde dormíamos. Me había quemado el chamorro. Bien me podía imaginar lo que sería estar en el infierno para siempre" (p. 60).

Viewed in light of these misfortunes, the curse episode acquires larger meaning. Hell is historical, not eternal, and La Raza is literally burning in it as it passively awaits its reward in the next world. The curse brings relief from the heat: one defiant act accomplishes more than endless supplication to an indifferent God.

In the last chapter the boy synthesizes the events of the past year in a long interior monologue. Everything finally comes to make sense. Feeling solidarity with the people, he wants to unite all the characters in one place and embrace them simultaneously. He realizes ". . . que en realidad no había perdido nada. Había encontrado. Encontrar y reencontrar y juntar. Relacionar esto con esto, eso con aquello, todo con todo. Eso era. Eso era todo" (p. 127). A final symbolic gesture further focuses his attention away from the individual reality and toward the social. Believing he sees a person who is looking at him, he waves his arm back and forth ". . . para que viera que él sabía que etaba allí" (p. 127).

Never at any point does he disavow what is probably the central act of work: his slander of the Deity. In spite of all his trauma, in the end he is content. He has cursed God and found happiness.

"The boy's discovery of self in the experience and the suffering of others is the antithesis of individualism and the affirmation of the value of collective identity" (Sommers 105). While *Pocho* is essentially the story of one person who finally chooses his own interests over those of his family and in so doing rejects the values of his heritage, *Y no se lo tragó la tierra*, as Professor Sommers explains, upholds the value of the group as the primary entity. Richard Rubio abandons religion because he identifies it with the collective ethos which prevents him from adopting the sort of individualism he has correctly identified as "American". Tomás Rivera's boy protagonist, on the other hand, rejects his spiritual legacy because it pacifies La Raza, thereby making it an easy target for exploitation by an economic system which, like God, does not care about poor people.

Paradoxically, anticlericalism is used to foster ends which are systematically and diametrically opposed. In *Pocho* it is used to support an individualist, assimilationist ideology which if generally accepted would do away with ethnic groups altogether. By contrast, anticlericalism in *Y no se lo tragó la tierra* affirms the collective spirit which is so subversive to main stream U. S. political ideology. It calls into question racism and exploitation and, therefore, advocates ethnic solidarity over assimilation.

In their political and philosophical implications, one would be hard pressed to find two works more completely at odds than *Y no se lo tragó la tierra* and *Pocho*. While the former is what one critic called "Altamente revolucionario" (Rodriguez 83), the latter provides not only a fictional rendering of the melting pot but an ideological justification as well.

NOTES

1. It could be argued, of course, that Richard need not have rejected his parents' religion in order to join the cult of the individual, that somehow the two are not mutually exclusive. This might be true in some historical sense, that is, apart from the logic of the novel, although I doubt it. But the point here is that Richard *sees* the two ideologies as incompatible and so concludes he must choose one or the other. Or, alternatively, the case could be made that he could have become a Protestant. Though perhaps philosophically feasible, it was, "in the Catholic town of Santa Clara," a choice not readily available to him (and the mother of the one Protestant friend he did have was a bigot).
2. Readers who are interested in the actual historical relations between the Chicano community and the Catholic church in Texas are referred to in an excellent article by José Roberto Juarez: "La Iglesia Católica y el Chicano en Sud Texas, 1836–1911." *Aztlán: Chicano Journal of the Social Sciences and the Arts*, IV (Fall 1973): 217–56.

LIST OF WORKS CITED

Bayes, Jane H. *Ideologies and Interest Group Politics*. Novato, CA: Chandler and Charp, 1982.

Rivera, Tomás. *Y no se lo tragó la tierra*. Berkeley: Editorial Justa, 1980.

Rodríguez, Juan. "La embestida contra la religiosidad en . . . *Y no se lo tragó la tierra*." *PCCLAS* [Pacific Coast Council on Latin American Studies] *Proceedings: Changing Perspectives in Latin America*, 3 (1974), 83–86.

Sommers, Joseph. "Interpreting Tomas Rivera." In *Modern Chicano* Writers. Ed. Joseph Sommers and Tomás Ibarra Fausto. Englewood Cliffs, NJ: Prentice Hall, 1979. pp. 94–107

Villarreal, José Antonio. *Pocho*. Garden City, NJ: Anchor Books, 1970.

THE RELATIONSHIP OF SPANISH LANGUAGE BACKGROUND TO ACADEMIC ACHIEVEMENT: A COMPARISON OF THREE GENERATIONS OF MEXICAN AMERICAN AND ANGLO-AMERICAN HIGH SCHOOL SENIORS

Raymond Buriel and Desdemona Cardoza

ABSTRACT

The present investigation examines the relationship of Spanish language background to achievement among first, second, and third generation Mexican high school seniors. A sample of Anglo-American students was also examined in order to determine if the effects of nonlinguistic socio-economic background variables on achievement were the same for students of both ethnic groups. The effects of students' and mothers' aspirations were also examined. Consistent with previous research, students' aspirations showed the strongest positive relationship to achievement for all groups of students. The next best set of predictors were linguistic variables. Although Spanish language background showed practically no relationship to achievement for first and second generation students, linguistic variables showed mixed effects for third generation students. In general, Spanish language effects on achievement were minimal thus arguing against the position that Spanish impedes the academic achievement of Mexican American students.

The retention of Spanish by Mexican Americans, has generated much debate over the effects of speaking this language on academic performance. On the one hand, advocates of linguistic assimilation have argued that since English fluency is a prerequisite for success in our traditional educational system, Mexican American children would be better-off speaking only English. Despite the seeming well-intended goal of this argument, it overlooks the fact that it is possible to be fluent in English and at the same time speak Spanish. More importantly though, is the fact that this argument completely ignores the bilingual reality of most Mexican American children. It is estimated that approximately 58 percent of all Mexican Americans live in bilingual homes where both English and Spanish are spoken in varying degrees (Macias, 1979). Only 14 percent of this population lives in exclusively English speaking households. Moreover, the proximity of Mexico as well as immigration from that country ensure that the use of Spanish by Mexican Americans will continue into the forseeable future. In short, the bilingual reality of most Mexican American children dictates that greater attention be paid to the effects of speaking Spanish on academic achievement before advocating a policy of linguistic assimilation.

Several studies have shown that deficiencies in English language skills are related to lower achievement among Mexican American children (see Matlock & Mace, 1973 for a review of articles). Implicit in many of these studies is the assumption that Spanish language background interferes with the development of English fluency. This assumption is made without having measured the students' knowledge of Spanish nor its relationship to academic achievement in English.

Contrary to assumptions about the damaging effects of Spanish, a growing body of literature suggests that knowledge of Spanish is positively related to achievement at all levels of education. For example, Henderson and Merritt (1968) investigated the environmental background of 80 Mexican American first-graders with either high or low potentials for school success. The mothers of these two groups of children were also interviewed in order to gather information on Activeness of Family and Intellectuality in the Home. To measure this nine environmental process variations previously identified as being related to school success were used. The high potential group, in addition to scoring higher on all nine environmental variables also scored higher on a test of Spanish vocabulary than the low potential group. The authors conclude that the "data seems to refute the common assumption that children from families that are 'most Mexican' in their behavior and outlook will have the most difficulty in school" (p. 105). A follow-up study of these same children at the end of the third grade confirmed the author's original conclusion (Henderson, 1972).

This also holds true at the college level. Several studies have demonstrated that Mexican American college students who speak Spanish stay in school longer and get better grades than those who are English monolingual. Long and Padilla (cited in Ramirez, 1971) investigated the bilingual antecedents of academic success among Spanish-surnamed graduate students at the University of New Mexico. The researchers compared the home language preference of two groups of students: (1) those who had successfully completed their graduate studies; and (2) those who had dropped out of the university. Results of their tabulations showed that 94 percent of the successful students were raised in bilingual homes compared to 8 percent of the unsuccessful students. On the basis of this finding, Long and Padilla concluded that bilingual students are better able to interact effectively with members of their own group and Anglo Americans.

In another study, García (1981) examined the effects of family and children's cultural maintenance upon children's achievement in college. Mexican American students from 13 colleges and universities in Texas were sampled. In all, 1,573 students responded to a questionnaire dealing with a wide variety of family-background, social-psychological, and achievement variables. Analysis of the data showed that being fluent in Spanish and coming from a Spanish-dominant home was positively associated with better grades in school. This finding held true even after important personality variables such as self-esteem and self-confidence were controlled (García, 1981).

A study by Gandara (1982) shows that the use of Spanish is prevalent among Mexican American women who have earned professional degrees. The 17 women in her study were from lower socioeconomic backgrounds and had succeeded in completing advanced graduate degrees. A structured two hour interview was used to elicit demographic and personal information that might explain these women's achievements. The data showed that in some ways these women were similar to high-achieving Anglo women. Their parents were nonauthoritarian in their disciplinary style and stressed early independence training. Still, there were some important and interesting differences between these women and high-achieving Anglos: "The majority of these women had not assimilated very much into North-American culture with respect to status variables. Almost all were Catholic, most were from large families (M=5.5 children), *most were bilingual or spoke only Spanish at home (77%) and most were first generation (70%)*" (p. 172; emphasis ours).

The above studies clearly demonstrate that speaking Spanish is not a liability to academic success in English. Nor is it incompatible with the development of English fluency. Of greater relevance to the present study, however, are the studies which focus on Spanish language background and achievement of Mexican American high school students.

The High School and Beyond study conducted by the National Opinion Research Center (Nielsen & Fernandez, 1981) provides comprehensive data to test the relationship of Spanish language background to school achievement. High school sophomores and seniors from public and private schools throughout the nation were sampled. In all, 58,728 students were studied, including 1,068 sophomores and 1,204 seniors who were of Mexican descent. All students completed a questionnaire covering a wide variety of family background variables, to identify the degrees of achievement between cultural integration and achievement variables. These students also took an extensive battery of psychological and achievement tests. Of particular relevance to the present discussion is the relationship between a set of cultural integration variables and a series of academic achievement measures. The cultural integration variables included Spanish usage, Spanish proficiency, and length of residence. Achievement was measured through educational aspirations, math achievement, reading achievement, and English vocabulary. Multiple regression analyses were conducted. This was done for both sophomores and seniors. Results of these analyses showed that for both classes, Spanish usage was associated with lower scores on all four achievement measures. However, Spanish proficiency was positively related to higher aspirations for both classes and also to greater math and vocabulary achievement for seniors. Although the results of Spanish usage and proficiency were mixed, one set of findings were highly consistent: the relationship of length of residence to achievement. For both sophomores and seniors, achievement decreased in all areas as length of residence in the United States increased.

Also using the HS&B data base, So and Chan (1982) found that both SES and language background have substantial and independent effects on reading achievement for both White and Hispanic students. However, the separate regression analyses show that SES has greater effects on the reading achievement of white students than on that of Hispanic students. In a subsequent study So (1982) reports that Hispanic youth who were limited English speaking students in bilingual elementary classrooms had higher high school reading and math achievement scores than Hispanic youth who were limited English proficient students in predominantly English or Spanish classrooms. This suggests the need to investigate factors which may mediate between elementary education and high school achievement testing to provide a more comprehensive understanding of the process leading to higher achievement.

The literature reviewed above focuses on the effects of cultural maintenance, specifically language skills, on academic achievement. Because an individual's success in the educational system is very often a prerequisite to occupational success, examination of the effects of these skills is extremely important.

The Nielsen and Fernandez (1981) study addresses another important issue, that is the covariation that exists between Spanish language usage and generational status. Indeed, their explanation for the length of residency findings allude to the possibility that generation and Spanish interact so as to affect student achievement. Nielsen and Fernandez propose a "ghettoization" hypothesis which argues that recent immigrants (first, and perhaps second generation) have not resided in this country long enough to have their achievement adversely affected by Anglo-American discrimination. They hypothesize further that "a more frequent use of Spanish by an individual, insofar as it indicates a more recent settlement and therefore less ghettoization, should be positively associated with achievement" (cited in Nielsen & Lerner, 1982, p. 2).

The purpose of the present study is to examine the relationship of Spanish language background including oral proficiency and literacy to academic achievement among first, second, and third generation Mexican Americans. The hypothesis under consideration is that Spanish language retention will affect achievement differently for different generational groups.

Methods

Data. The data used for this study are from the first phase of the High School and Beyond (HS&B) longitudinal study. This national survey is particularly useful for investigating questions pertaining to the multifaceted effects of ethnicity on educational and socioeconomic outcomes. One of the features of the survey is the fact that Hispanics were oversampled, making it the first large data bases of its kind. Also, special attention was paid to the collection of data on language minority populations (Nielsen & Fernandez, 1981; So, 1982). About 11,300 students who gave a non-English response to any of five language questions in the general questionnaire were asked detailed questions regarding their language experiences and behavior. Additionally, detailed information on immigration and ethnicity, as well as educational achievement and employment data, was also included.

Sample. As indicated earlier, a primary focus of the present study was to examine the relationship of Spanish language background to achievement among Mexican American students. Consequently a subsample of senior level students identifying themselves specifically as Mexican, Mexican American or Chicano, were selected. The sample was restricted to three regions: (1) the Pacific region, including California, Oregon, Washington, Alaska and Hawaii, (2) the mountain region which included Montana, Idaho, Wyoming, Colorado, New Mexico, Arizona, Utah and Nevada, and (3) the West South Central region including Arkansas, Louisiana, Oklahoma and Texas. The sample was limited to these regions for two reasons. First, over 85 percent of all Mexican Americans living in the United States reside in these three regions. Second, it was felt that in order to control for possible regional variations associated with living in the midwest versus the southwest, the regions should be restricted to those in the southwest. A subsample of Anglo-American students from these same regions, was also selected in order to determine if the effects of non-linguistic background variables (i.e., aspiration and socioeconomic variables) are the same for students of both ethnic groups. Anglo-American status was determined by students identifying themselves as white and of European background.

Language variables. As previously mentioned substantial language background information was available for these students. Respondents who answered "Spanish" to at least one of five questions (first language spoken; other language spoken as a child; current usual household language), were classified as being of Spanish language background. These students were then asked a series of questions regarding their Spanish proficiency (oral and literacy) and their Spanish usage.

Relevant to the present study are the Spanish proficiency indicators. Past research has indicated that the concept of Spanish proficiency may be improved when represented as two separate constructs; oral proficiency and literacy (Fishman, 1969; Fernandez, 1980; Cardoza & Hirano-Nakanishi, 1984). In this vein, the responses to the questions "How well do you understand Spanish?" and "How well do you speak Spanish?" were combined to form the variable of Spanish oral proficiency. The two questions pertaining to literacy skills "How well do you read Spanish?" and "How well do you write Spanish?" were combined to form the Spanish literacy variable. The possible responses to these questions consisted of a four point scale ranging from very well to not at all. For both the oral proficiency and literacy variables, the responses were standardized and summed to form the final variable.

The other two language variables used were mother tongue and home language environment. Mother tongue consisted of two items: "What was the first language you spoke when you were a child?" and "What other language did you speak when you were a child?" Responses to these two items were crosstabulated to form a continuous variable which had four values: (1) English monolingual, (2) English dominant bilingual, (3) Spanish dominant bilingual, and (4) Spanish monolingual. The variable home language environment was calculated in the same manner using the two questions "What language do people in your home usually speak?" and "What other language is spoken in your home?"

Family education and income variables. Both father's and mother's educational attainment were included in the analysis as possible predictors of academic achievement. Students' responses to the question "What was the highest level of education your mother/father completed?" ranged from less than high school graduation to obtaining an advanced professional degree. Family income, broken down into intervals of sevenths, was also included.

Aspirations variables. Students' aspirations were measured by their response to the question, "As things stand now, how far in school do you think you will get?" There were nine response categories ranging from "less than high school" to "Ph.D., M.D. or other advanced degree." Responses were scored on a scale of 1–9 with higher scores in the direction of more desired education. Mother's aspirations were ascertained from students' responses to the question "As things stand now, how far in school does your mother think you will get?" The same nine point response categories were used to score mothers' aspirations.

Achievement measures. Four achievement variables were used as the outcome measures in this study. These consisted of scores on a math test, a reading test and vocabulary test. The scores were standardized and summed to form a total achievement variable.

Generation. Respondents were considered to be first generation if they

73

indicated that they were not born in the United States. They were second generation if they responded that they were born in the United States, but either their mother or father were not. They were considered third generation if they and both of their parents were U.S. born.

Results

The means and standard deviations for the language, family socioeconomic, aspiration and achievement variables are presented in Table 1. These are presented for the three generations of Mexican American Students, as well as for the Anglo-American.

Table 1

Means and Standard Deviations for Achievement, Socioeconomic Aspiration and Language Variables

				Mexican American						Anglo-American		
	1st generation			2nd generation			3rd generation					
	N	Mean	SD	N	Mean	SD	N	Mean	SD	N	Mean	SD
Achievement Variables												
Composite Achievement Score	117	46.67	7.62	157	46.93	7.92	768	47.57	8.05	961	53.73	8.38
Math Test Standardized Score	119	54.77	9.37	158	47.17	9.77	770	47.12	9.87	962	52.83	9.69
Reading Test Standardized Score	121	45.77	8.84	159	46.28	9.51	773	47.99	9.66	968	53.52	10.16
Vocabulary Test Standardized Score	120	48.06	9.68	160	37.15	8.95	774	47.60	9.45	972	53.78	10.00
Socioeconomic Variables												
Father's Education[a]	103	1.73	1.45	125	1.61	1.19	674	2.03	1.39	850	3.30	1.81
Mother's Education[a]	110	1.46	0.99	127	1.55	1.02	755	1.82	1.11	973	2.83	1.44
Family Income by Sevenths[c]	125	2.70	1.41	154	3.02	1.60	804	3.42	1.70	1009	4.31	1.78
Aspiration Variables												
Student's School Aspirations[b]	137	3.89	1.53	171	3.98	1.49	897	3.93	1.48	1092	4.34	1.51
Mother's School Aspirations[b]	106	4.75	1.54	138	4.51	1.50	718	4.48	1.54	867	4.78	1.44
Language Variables												
Spanish Oral Proficiency[d]	130	3.59	1.07	158	3.43	1.04	760	3.00	1.40	—	—	—
Spanish Literacy[e]	130	3.17	1.48	159	2.85	1.62	759	2.34	1.78	—	—	—
Home Language[f]	133	3.14	0.77	159	2.89	0.78	781	2.47	0.74	—	—	—
Mother Tongue[g]	133	3.69	0.57	164	3.12	0.75	778	2.27	0.97	—	—	—

[a]Parent's level of education is a 1 to 9 scale ranging from less than high school graduate to Ph.D.
[b]School aspiration is a 1 to 9 scale ranging from less than high school graduate to Ph.D.
[c]Family income was measured on a 7 point interval scale ranging from <6,999 to >38,000.
[d]Oral proficiency is a combination of understanding and speaking Spanish (1) not at all, (2) not very well, (3) pretty well, and (4) very well.
[e]Literacy is a combination of reading and writing Spanish (1) not at all, (2) not very well, (3) pretty well, and (4) very well.
[f]Home language was derived from a cross-tabulation of language spoken producing the values of (1) English monolingual, (2) English dominant, (3) Spanish dominant, and (4) Spanish monolingual.
[g]Mother tongue was derived from a cross-tabulation of language spoken as a child producing the values of (1) English monolingual, (2) English dominant, (3) Spanish dominant, and (4) Spanish monolingual.

Separate regression equations using a forward stepwise solution were calculated for the three generational groups and the Anglo-American group using the four achievement variables as dependent variables. Table 2 presents the results of the dependent variable representing the composite score of the three achievement tests. For first generation Mexican American students, the only variable which entered significantly into the equation was student aspiration, accounting for about 31 percent of the variance.

For second generation, student aspiration was again the most significant predictor accounting for about 32 percent of the variation in the total achievement measure. The second variable significantly contributing to the explanation of variation in the total achievement measure was Spanish literacy. This variable is positively related to achievement meaning that as literacy skills in Spanish increase, so does achievement as measured by this composite indicator. Spanish oral proficiency was the final predictor. This variable loaded in a negative direction indicating that as Spanish oral proficiency increased, achievement decreased.

Table 2

Predictors of Total Achievement Among First, Second and Third Generation Mexican American and Anglo-American Students

Mexican American		
1st generation		
Student's Aspirations	8.50	.317
2nd generation		
Student's Aspirations	9.35	.317
Spanish Literacy Proficiency	5.52	.351
Oral Proficiency	–6.91	.389
3rd generation		
Student's Aspirations	6.96	.230
Mother Tongue	–4.96	.230
Father's Education	1.86	.293
Anglo-American		
Student's Aspirations	6.31	.216
Mother's Education	1.97	.239
Family income by Sevenths	1.58	.249

For third generation Mexican American students, their educational aspiration is still the main predictor, explaining 23 percent of the variance. Mother tongue enters second, revealing that students from a monolingual English background fair better on this achievement measure. Finally, father's education, explaining an additional 6 percent of the variance.

For the Anglo-American students aspiration was again the most important predictor of achievement, explaining approximately 22 percent of the variation. Mother's education and family income were also significant, increasing the variance explained to 24 and 25 percent respectively.

The results of the regression analyses for the measure of math achievement are presented in Table 3. For both first and second generation, student aspiration was the only significant predictor. For first generation it explains approximately 35 percent of the variance and in second generation it drops to 26 percent. For third generation the variables home language and mother tongue are also entered, increasing the variance explained by about 2 percent.

For the Anglo-American student a similar pattern to that of the total achievement variable surfaced. Student aspiration, mother's education and family income were the only variables which loaded significantly. Combined, they explained close to 25 percent of the variation in this dependent measure.

Table 4 presents the results of the regression analyses for the reading achievement variable. As with math, for first and second generation the only significant predictor variable was student aspiration. For third generation, in addition to student aspiration, three language variables contributed significantly to the explanation of variance. These variables were mother tongue, Spanish oral proficiency, and Spanish literacy. Students with a mother tongue of English, and no Spanish language background tended to score higher on the reading achievement test. Additionally students who reported greater oral proficiency in Spanish tended not to do as well on this achievement measure. However, students reporting greater literacy skills in Spanish tended to score higher on the reading test.

For the Anglo-American group, student aspiration was the only significant predictor, accounting for approximately 12 percent of the variance.

The results of the regression analyses for the vocabulary achievement test are shown in Table 5. For first generation Mexican Americans the important predictors are student's and mother's aspiration, together accounting for approximately 23 percent of the variance. For second generation, student aspiration was the most

Table 3

Predictors of Math Achievement Among First, Second and Third Generation Mexican American Students and Anglo-American Students

Mexican American	Math B	Incremental R^2
1st generation		
Student's Aspirations	3.57	.348
2nd generation		
Student's Aspirations	3.87	.262
3rd generation		
Student's Aspirations	3.12	.239
Home Language	−1.70	.268
Mother Tongue	−1.13	.278
Anglo-American		
Student's Aspirations	2.45	.209
Mother's Education	.862	.234
Family income by Sevenths	.597	.244

Table 4

Predictors of Reading Achievement Among First, Second and Third Generation Mexican American Students and Anglo-American Students

Mexican American	Reading B	Incremental R^2
1st generation		
Student's Aspirations	2.3	.130
2nd generation		
Student's Aspirations	3.1	.193
3rd generation		
Student's Aspirations	2.0	.121
Mother Tongue	−1.6	.174
Oral Proficiency	−1.5	.186
Spanish Literacy Proficiency	.826	.200
Anglo-American		
Student's Aspirations	2.24	.115

important predictor (explaining 25 percent of the variance). Oral proficiency loaded in a negative direction indicated that as ability in understanding and speaking Spanish increased, vocabulary achievement decreased. The opposite is true, however, for literacy skills in Spanish. As these skills increased student performance on the vocabulary test also increased. For the third generation, student aspiration and father's education jointly explained 15 percent of the variation in the vocabulary measure. Mother tongue entered in a negative direction, increasing the R^2 by 1 percent, indicating that monolingual English students score higher on the vocabulary achievement test. For the Anglo-American students, student's aspiration, family income and mother's education account for about 18 percent of the variance.

Table 5

Predictors of Vocabulary Achievement Among First, Second and Third Generation Mexican American Students and Anglo-American Students

Mexican American	Reading B	Incremental R^2
1st generation		
Student's Aspirations	4.55	.168
Mother's Aspirations	2.44	.234
2nd generation		
Student's Aspirations	2.93	.253
Spanish Literacy	2.10	.293
Oral Proficiency	−2.63	.336
3rd generation		
Student's Aspirations	1.86	.120
Home Language	.91	.150
Mother Tongue	−1.26	.166
Anglo-American		
Student's Aspirations	1.81	.134
Family income by Sevenths	.862	.169
Mother's Education	.831	.183

Discussion

Results of this study show that personal aspirations are by far the most potent predictors of academic achievement for both Mexican and Anglo-American students. The next best set of predictors differs according to ethnicity and generational status. In terms of ethnicity, socioeconomic variables account for a substantial percentage of achievement variance for Anglo-American students. However, socioeconomic variables do not add to the explanation of variance for Mexican Americans. With respect to generation, results indicate a differential relationship of Spanish language variables to achievement for the three generations of Mexican American students. In general, Spanish language variables showed a) no relationship whatsoever to achievement for first generation students; b) a modest and mixed relationship exclusively for vocabulary achievement among second generation students; and, c) a moderate, and sometimes mixed relationship to all measures of achievement for third generation students. Overall the trend was for an increasing and more diversified relationship of Spanish to achievement across three generations.

An examination of the findings for the three generations suggest that Spanish background variables have a long term, delayed effect on students' achievement (see Table 6). That is, even though first generation students come from predominantly Spanish oriented environments, Spanish language variables have *no* effect on these students' achievement. By contrast, third generation students exhibit the strongest relationship of linguistic factors to achievement. Moreover, the results are both positive and negative depending on the type of achievement test and nature of the language variable. On the minus side, Spanish mother tongue is consistently related to lower achievement for these students. Since the trend is for Spanish usage to wane over time, third generation students with a Spanish mother tongue probably represent an unusual group of individuals. On the plus side, third generation students with Spanish literacy have higher reading scores.

Table 6

Positive and Neutral Effects of Language Variables on First, Second and Third Generation Mexican American Students

	Math	Reading	Vocabulary	
Mother Tongue	0	0	0	
Home Language	0	0	0	
Oral Proficiency	0	0	0	1st Generation
Literacy	0	0	0	
	Math	Reading	Vocabulary	
Mother Tongue	0	0	0	
Home Language	0	0	0	
Oral Proficiency	0	0	−	2nd Generation
Literacy	0	0	+	
	Math	Reading	Vocabulary	
Mother Tongue	−	−	−	
Home Language	−	0	0	
Oral Proficiency	0	−	0	3rd Generation
Literacy	0	+	0	

It is interesting to speculate on the positive relationships of Spanish literacy to reading achievement. Because these students are third generation, their ability to read and write in Spanish can probably be attributed to the educational system in the United States. They either have taken Spanish in high school, or have been involved in some type of bilingual program which promotes literacy in both English and Spanish. Regardless of how these abilities are achieved, the fact still remains that their effect is positive on academic achievement. This could be used as an important factor in strengthening the argument for bilingual education programs. In other words, learning to read in two languages, rather than impeding academic growth, enhances it.

The delayed effects of Spanish on achievement reflect aspects of both Buriel's (1984) Cultural Integration hypothesis and Nielsen and Fernandez' (1981) Ghettoization hypothesis. According to Buriel, Mexican immigration is selective in nature and is principally motivated by a desire for change, upward mobility, and achievement. This position argues that the highly achievement oriented values of immigrants are an integral part of immigrant Mexican American culture in the United States. Individuals who are well integrated in this immigrant culture are likely to express these values in their behavior. Moreover, for these individuals learning English is recognized as a prerequisite for achieving their aspirations. However, strong ethnic pride prescribes that learning English should not take place at the expense of Spanish. The result is a bilingual individual with high aspirations for success. In terms of our own sample, first and second generation students are most likely to be exposed to the positive effects of traditional Mexican American culture since both are the offspring of immigrant parents. Although these students come from predominantly Spanish speaking environments, their high aspirations for success override any potentially limiting effects of their non-English background. This may be why achievement was explained almost entirely by personal aspirations for students from immigrant families.

By the third, and subsequent generations, one of two situations is likely to characterize the families of these students. On the one hand, they have successfully built on the gains of the previous generations and become integrated into United States society. This being the case, they are unlikely to have Spanish as a mother tongue. Although Spanish may be spoken at home, it is to a far lesser degree than in first and second generations families. Still, ethnic pride encourages the learning of Spanish which now takes place in school as a foreign language. Since foreign language courses are often a prerequisite for higher education, these students are also likely to be high achievers. This explains the positive relationship of Spanish literacy to achievement for third generation students. This scenario is the logical outcome of the cultural integration hypothesis. That is, adherence to the achievement oriented values of immigrants leads eventually to social mobility in this society. After several generations, middle class achievement inertia may replace immigrant values as the impetus for continued success.

The Ghettoization hypothesis, on the other hand, describes the situation of third generation students whose families have not been economically mobile. These families are likely to find themselves in low income environments (barrios or ghettos) that are heavily Spanish speaking. This being the case they are likely to report a Spanish mother tongue and use Spanish at home (although to a lesser extent than immigrant families). Since students in these families observe that economic mobility has by-passed their grandparents' and parents' generations they may be less optimistic about their own chances for success than children of recent immigrants. Although their stated aspirations may still be high, their expectations for achieving them may be low (Buriel, Calzada, & Vasquez 1982). This disjunction between aspirations and expectations may weaken the relationship of aspirations to achievement. This might explain why aspirations contributed less to the variance of achievement for third generation students relative to their first and second generation counterparts. All things considered, these individuals' use of Spanish probably reflects a lack of integration, and perhaps even enthusiasm, in United States society which in turn shows up in lower achievement. Thus, the achievement values of immigrants are lost although Spanish, in some form, remains.

It should be noted here that the third generation students in this sample have probably not been ghettoized in the full sense of the concept. Past research has demonstrated that among Hispanic dropouts, 60 percent leave school before the tenth grade (Nielsen & Fernandez 1981). Consequently, the students represented in this sample are those who are talented and determined enough to survive through high school beyond the tenth grade. Instead their behavior has probably been only remotely influenced by ghettoization. The full impact of ghettoization is probably reflected in the lives of those students who dropped out and never made it through high school.

By and large though, Spanish background variables are only intermittently related to achievement as is apparent from an examination of Table 6. The preponderance of neutral effects (0's) that show up in this table clearly indicate that, at least for these high school seniors, Spanish background bears very little relationship to their achievement scores.

One possible explanation for these findings is that the relationship of Spanish to achievement expresses itself earlier in students' academic careers. Thus, students who were adversely affected by their Spanish language background may have already dropped out of school. This explanation, however, is hard pressed to explain why so many students from predominantly Spanish speaking environments—like first and second generation students—get to be high school seniors.

Another possible explanation is that the presumed deleterious effects of Spanish have been overstated and, in fact, there is very little or no relationship of Spanish to achievement in either a positive or negative direction. It is our contention that this is most likely the case. The overriding predictor for all three generational groups as well as for the Anglo-American group was student aspiration. Students with high educational aspirations tended to do better on all achievement variables. By comparison, the contribution of the language variables, whether positively or negatively, was quite small. This was also true with regard to the socioeconomic variables for third generation Mexican American students, as well as the Anglo-American students. The findings of this study do not support the notion that retention and use of Spanish somehow has deleterious effect on the academic achievement of Hispanic students. It appears that Spanish language background bears very little relationship to achievement for Mexican American students.

REFERENCES

Buriel, R. "Integration with Traditional Mexican-American Culture and Sociocultural Adjustment." In J. L. Martinez, Jr. and R. H. Mendoza (Eds.) *Chicano Psychology* (2nd ed.), New York: Academic Press, 1984.

Buriel, R., Calzada, S., & Vasquez, R. (1982). "The relationship of traditional Mexican American culture to adjustment and delinquency among three generations of Mexican American adolescents." *Hispanic Journal of Behavioral Sciences, 4* 41–55.

Cardoza, D., & Hirano-Nakanishi, M. (1984). *Conceptualizing Language Factors in Survey Data: A Look at the High School & Beyond.* Los Alamitos, CA: National Center for Bilingual Research.

Fernandez, R. (1980). Appendix D: Selected analyses of the pretest data. In Nielsen, F. (Ed.), *Hispanic Youth in U.S. Schools: A Design for Analysis.* Report to the National Center for Education Statistics. Chicago, IL: National Opinion Research Center.

Fishman, J. A. (1969). "A Sociolinguistic Census of a Bilingual Neighborhood." *American Journal of Sociology, 75* (3), 323–339.

Gandara, P. (1982). "Passing Through the Eye of the Media: High Achieving Chicanos." *Hispanic Journal of Behavioral Sciences, 4* 167–179.

García, H. D. C. (1981). *Bilingualism, Confidence, and College Achievement.* (Report No. 318). Center for Socio Organization of Schools, Johns Hopkins University, Baltimore, MD.

Henderson, R. W. (1972). *"Environmental Predictors of Academic Performance of Disadvantaged Mexican-American Children." Journal of Consulting and Clinical Psychology, 38,* 297.

Henderson, R. W. & Merritt, C. G. (1968). *"Environmental Backgrounds of Mexican American Children with Different Potentials of School Success." Journal of Social Psychology, 75,* 101–106.

Macias, R. (1979). *Mexican/Chicano Sociolinguistic Behavior and Language Policy in the United States.* Unpublished doctoral dissertation, Georgetown University, Washington, D.C.

Matlock, J. H., & Mace, D. J. (1973). *"Language Characteristics of Mexican American Children: Implications for Assessment." Journal of School Psychology, 11* (4), 365–386.

Nielson, F., & Fernandez, R. M. (1981). *Hispanic Students in American High Schools: Background Characteristics and Achievement.* Contractor's Report to the National Center for Educational Statistics. Washington, D.C.: U.S. Government Printing Office.

Nielson, F., & Lerner, S. J. (1982). "Language Skills and School Achievement in Bilingual Hispanics." (Mimeo). Unpublished manuscript. University of North Carolina, Department of Sociology, Chapel Hill.

Ramirez, M. (1971). "The Relationship of Acculturation to Educational Achievement and Psychological Adjustment in Chicano Children and Adolescents: A Review of the Literature." *El Grito: A Journal of contemporary Mexican-American Thought, 4,* 21–28.

So, A. (1982). *The High School and Beyond Data Set: Its Relevance for Bilingual Education Research.* Los Alamitos, CA: National Center for Bilingual Research.

So, A., & Chan, K. S. (1982). *What Matters? The Relative Impact of Language Background and Socioeconomic Status on Reading Achievement.* Los Alamitos, CA: National Center for Bilingual Research.

THE CAUSES OF NATURALIZATION AND NON-NATURALIZATION AMONG MEXICAN IMMIGRANTS

Celestino Fernández

ABSTRACT

This chapter reports on a study of the causes of naturalization and non-naturalization among Mexican immigrants. Since the beginning of this century, Mexican immigrants (legal "permanent resident aliens") have had the lowest rate of naturalization of any immigrant group, including groups from countries near the United States. A variety of factors have contributed to this low rate which can be grouped into three categories; background characteristics (e.g., education, socioeconomic status, age, gender, and occupation), structural conditions (e.g., discriminatory immigration and naturalization laws and policies, lack of outreach programs for Mexican immigrants, proximity to home country, structure of naturalization requirements, and costs and benefits of naturalization), and cultural forces (e.g., family ties, peer pressure from friends, natural identity, religion, perceived costs and benefits to naturalization). Data for this study were gathered through in-depth oral case histories of naturalized Mexican immigrants as well as Mexican immigrants eligible for naturalization but who had not become United Sates citizens. Our findings suggest that outreach programs to assist Mexican immigrants can be very effective by taking advantage of the knowledge gained through this and other studies that look at the ways in which Mexican immigrants perceive naturalization.

Since the beginning of this century, Mexican immigrants have had the lowest rate of naturalization of any immigrant group. This factor is a critical issue for Mexican Americans because only full-fledged citizens may participate in the political process. Thus, this pattern of non-naturalization has created a pool of disenfranchised legal residents in the United States. This study was undertaken to ascertain the reasons why Mexican immigrants tend to refrain from American citizenship. It focuses on a variety of factors which have been grouped into three categories; background characteristics, structural conditions and cultural forces. Specifically, it focuses on how Mexican immigrants perceive citizenship and their residence in the United States.

Every immigrant admitted into the United States as a permanent resident is a potential candidate for naturalization. Immigrants from different countries, however, naturalizize at varying rates. A study conducted in 1973 found that of those admitted for permanent residence between 1960 and 1965 about 25% had chosen to become naturalized. Of those naturalized, the variation among nationalities was quite large. The highest rate was among Rumanians with over 70% compared to a low of under 3% for Mexicans (Interagency Task Force on Immigration Policy, 1979).

This pattern of refraining from American citizenship is historical for Mexican immigrants. Walker (1928) found that of the 934 persons to become naturalized between 1926 and 1928 in the counties of Los Angeles, Orange and Riverside, only five were Mexican. It is important to note that of these three counties in Southern California the greatest proportion of the foreign-born population was Mexican. During 1959–1965, Grebler (1966), reported variances of 2.4 to 5 percent for Mexicans and 27 to 33 percent for all other immigrants. A later research project (Orozco, 1978) traced rates of naturalization for various immigrant groups from 1968 to 1976. Annual rates of naturalization for Mexican nationals varied from 3.9 to 5.9 percent as compared with 30.2 to 50.6 percent for non-Mexican immigrants. More recently, using data from the 1979 Chicano Survey, García (1981) found that of Mexican-born respondents only 14% had become naturalized. Baca and Bryan (1980) reported that, from a sample of 1,400 undocumented Mexican immigrants, only 15% would choose to become U.S. citizens while 77% would prefer permanent residence status only.

A variable which may be a contributing factor to the variation of naturalization among nationalities is the proximity of the mother country to the United States. This hypothesis was examined by reviewing data from annual INS reports. Canadians, who share a contiguous border with the United States, are about one-half as likely as immigrants in general to become American citizens. They are, however, almost twice as likely as Mexicans to naturalize. Cuban immigrants, on the other hand, have one of the highest rates of naturalization. Thus, other significant factors, associated with naturalization, must be examined if the relatively low naturalization rate for Mexican immigrants is to be understood.

This pattern is a critical issue since it allows for a large group of Mexican Americans living in the United States to be disenfranchised from the sociopolitical structure. While the laws apply equally to all residents, only citizens have the right to vote. Analysis of data collected by the Southwest Voter Registration Education Project and figures of the 1980 Census show that nearly 25% of all Mexican Americans in this country are disenfranchised legal permanent residents rendered devoid of political power by their non-citizen status. Two situations which will add a significant number of Mexicans to this group of politically marginal residents are: 1) the population growth rate which by 1990 will make Hispanics the largest minority group, and 2) the amnesty portion of the Immigration Reform Bill passed by the 99th Congress in December 1986.

Data for this study was generated from in-depth oral case histories. Interviews, averaging three hours, were conducted with 60 Mexican immigrants; 20 of which were naturalized and 40 of which were eligible for citizenship but who had not gone through the process of naturalization. Fifty of the interviews were conducted in Los Angeles, California (primarily in East Los Angeles). Los Angeles was selected because 1980 Census data indicated that 94.1% of East Los Angeles residents are of Hispanic origin or descent. Moreover, 45.2% of these people were foreign born, most of them in Mexico. Ten interviews were conducted in Tucson, Arizona, for the purposes of comparison. Since no differences were found when the data were analyzed, the samples were combined into a single sample. The sample took into consideration: sex, age, educational levels, length of residency and major job categories. Respondents were interviewed in the language of their choice (English/ Spanish) by fully bilingual individuals. Interviews were open dialogue which gave informants the opportunity to express freely their sentiments, thoughts, beliefs and experiences relative to naturalization.

Analysis of the data focused on synthesising the ethnographies and oral case histories in order to look for patterns. This type of qualitative analysis produced many factors which have been categorized into three broad groups: background characteristics, structural conditions, and cultural forces.

Results

Although there are many factors associated with a person's decision to naturalize, they can be categorized into three broad groups: background character- istics, structural conditions, and cultural forces.

Background Characteristics

Several background characteristics (age, sex, level of education, occupation, and length of time living in the United States) were found to be related to naturalization, as discussed below. Generally, although not in all cases, our findings are consistent with those reported in other studies (García, 1981; Grebler, 1966; and Ramírez, 1979). Our data, however, permit further analysis and interpretation than was possible by other researchers. Moreover, our study provides new insights into the ways in which background variables are associated with naturalization.

1. Level of Education

Both García (1981) and Ramírez (1979) found that education is positively associated with naturalization. In other words, as years of schooling increases so does the likelihood of becoming a citizen. Our findings are consistent with this relation- ship; we found a positive association between education and having obtained citizenship. In fact, it was very difficult to locate naturalized citizens with little or no education while we had no trouble locating non-naturalized Mexican immigrants at this level of education. Yet, the association between the education variable and naturalization is more complex. While Mexican immigrants with fewer years of formal schooling are less likely than those with more years to become citizens, they are not less favorably disposed to the possibility of becoming citizens. We found many individuals with little or no education who expressed a very strong interest in becoming citizens. Yet, given their marginality from mainstream American culture, it is very unlikely that such individuals will become citizens. Thus, the real issue is not years of education per se but the structural factors (e.g., socioeconomic status, language, access to networks and offices) that prevent the less educated from obtaining citizenship.

2. Age

As reported by Grebler (1966) and Ramírez (1979), younger Mexican immigrants are much more likely to become citizens than older individuals. For

Mexicans, unlike other immigrant groups, if an immigrant has not become a United States citizen by the time he/she reaches the age of 55, the chances of that person becoming naturalized decrease drastically, to almost zero.

The 20–50 age group has the highest probability of becoming citizens. Of course, one should keep in mind that an individual must have reached the age of 18 before he/she can file for citizenship. Yet, if one is under 18, one can automatically become a citizen if one's parents are naturalized. It is interesting to note, however, that relatively few Mexicans (about 10 percent of those naturalized) obtain citizenship through their parents.

The younger persons we interviewed tended to support the view that citizenship was more convenient for their age group and that perhaps it was something that should not be pursued by older individuals. In talking about his parents, one respondent summarized this attitude as follows:

> No, ellos así estan bien, ellos no la necesitan. La ciudadanía más bien es para los jovenes.
>
> No, they're fine like that, they don't need it. Citizenship is for younger people.

3. Gender

Research findings on the relationship between sex and naturalization have been mixed. Ramírez (1979), for example, reports that males are more likely than females to become citizens. Baca and Bryan (1980) found that Mexican men and women were equally likely to prefer permanent resident alien status over other forms (including United States citizenship). Grebler (1966) found no sex difference when looking at the number of Mexicans who became naturalized during a five year period. On the other hand, the 1980 Annual Report to the Immigration and Naturalization Service shows that Mexican women outnumbered Mexican men in becoming citizens, 56 percent and 44 percent, respectively (INS, Annual Report, 1980).

Our study went beyond previous research in assessing the relationship between sex and naturalization and provides insights which indicate that the relationship is quite complex. Basically women appear to be more practical and realistic in their approach to citizenship than men. In short, women were much more interested in becoming citizens; and they were more likely to have seriously thought about the possibility of going through the naturalization process.

We encountered a number of women who very frankly told us that they were ready to become citizens but that their husbands objected to it. A few women even said that they were getting ready to become citizens (they were actually enrolled in preparation classes) but without their husbands' knowledge. We did not encounter any man who stated, or even implied, that his wife was against his becoming naturalized. On the contrary, women were quite supportive of their husbands seeking citizenship. In fact in most cases where both the husband and wife had become citizens, it was the wife who had provided the initial impetus and it was she who had taken the lead and provided sustained support during the process.

Some of the most interesting interviews were those in which both spouses were participating in the discussion. A few women put their husbands on the spot, for example, by stating very directly that she very much wanted to become a citizen but that, "él no me deja" (he will not let me).

4. Occupation

Our findings regarding the relationship between occupation and naturalization are very similar to those for education. While individuals in higher status occupations are more likely to become citizens than those in unskilled positions, they are not any more likely to want to become citizens. In other words, unskilled laborers generally want to become citizens in roughly the same numbers as do persons in professional positions but, like for unschooled immigrants, it becomes much more difficult for unskilled workers to go through the process because they do not have access to networks and/or organizations that will help them learn about the requirements and prepare for the naturalization examination.

5. Length of Residence

With few exceptions, an immigrant must have resided in the United States as a permanent resident alien for five years before becoming eligible for citizenship. As noted earlier, Mexican immigrants not only naturalize at lower rates than other nationalities, but they also tend to wait longer before they become citizens.

In general, length of residence is positively related to the attainment of citizenship status; the longer one has resided in the United States the more likely that one will have become a citizen. This finding is consistent with other research (e.g., García, 1981), however, as with age, there seems to be an upper limit. It was not uncommon, for example, to find persons who had resided in the United States, as legal residents, for over 30 to 40 years and who have decided that they will never become citizens. These respondents frequently stated that, "esas cosas son para los jovenes" (that—naturalization—is for younger people).

Many of these people still held onto the dream of someday returning to Mexico (permanently, to live). One man stated that he and his wife could not return now because their children needed them here,

> . . . pero tal vez cuando ellos ya no nos necesiten más, tal vez podamos entonces regresar.
>
> . . . but that perhaps when they (our children) don't need us anymore, maybe then we can return.

The irony of this situation was that "the children" were all grown adults and only one still lived at home. In reality, the parents "needed" the children as much as or more than the children needed the parents. This rationalization, however, allowed the dream of returning to Mexico to continue to live in their minds.

Structural Conditions

This category incorporates several historical and contemporary factors that have played a major role in the non-naturalization of Mexican immigrants.

1. Immigration and Naturalization Laws

The history of immigration and naturalization laws clearly indicates that discrimination based on national origin has been common in the United States. For example, a) discrimination based on national origin became part of United States immigration laws beginning with the Chinese Exclusion Act of May 6, 1882; b) the Gentlemen's Agreement of 1907 limited the entry of Japanese labor; and c) the Act of 1917 set up the Asia-Pacific Triangle by degrees of latitude and longitude and excluded all persons born in this proscribed area as inadmissible to the United States, (this Act enlarged the scope of persons banned on the basis of national origin or race to include Hindus and other Asians). In addition, the Act of May 19, 1921, introduced the concept of general quota based upon nationality. The Act of May 26, 1924, made the national quotas even more restrictive by basing them on two percent of the number of individuals of each nationality in the United States as enumerated by the 1890 Census. This new measure, in effect, gave preferential treatment to northern Europeans and discriminated against southern and eastern Europeans.

Naturalization law is also filled with discriminatory regulations. The very first naturalization act, the Act of March 26, 1790, provided the naturalization of free, *white* aliens with two or more years of residence in the United States, thus, excluding most of the world's population. Eighty years later, pursuant to the Act of July 14, 1870, persons of African "nativity" and descent became eligible for citizenship. However, the Act of May 6, 1882, prohibited any State or United States Court from admitting Chinese to citizenship. This ban was not repealed until 60 years later, with the Act of December 17, 1943.

The Act of October 14, 1940, made Eskimos and Aleutians eligible for citizenship. Filipinos became eligible in 1946 and Guamanians in 1950. It was not until the Act of June 27, 1952, that discrimination for naturalization based on race was removed. The act stated that:

> The right of a person to become a naturalized citizen of the United States shall not be denied or abridged because of race or sex or because such person is married.

The experiences of Mexican immigrants have ranged from merely crossing the border in 1880 and paying a nominal fee of 50 cents to become a full-fledged American citizen to denial of citizenship status because they were neither white nor of African descent (Reisler, 1976). The Bureau viewed Mexican immigrants as desirable workers but undesirable as potential citizens. In 1910, for example, the *Report of the Immigration Commission* stated the following (quoted in Acuña, 1972:132):

> The assimilative qualities of the Mexicans are slight. Because of backward educational facilities in their native land and a constitutional prejudice on the part of the peones toward school attendance, the immigrants of this race have among them a larger percentage of illiterates than is found among any race immigrating to the western country in any considerable manner.

> Because of a lack of thrift and a tendency to regard public relief as "pension" . . . many Mexican families in time of industrial depression become public charges . . .

> Thus it is evident that, in the case of the Mexican, he is less desirable as a citizen than as a laborer. The permanent additions to the population, however, are much smaller than the number who immigrate for work.

2. Immigration and Naturalization Service

Historically, INS has not provided information and outreach programs to assist Mexican immigrants as it has for other groups, e.g., Cubans, Vietnamese and Northern and Western Europeans. Generally, the agency has taken the attitude that

Mexicans immigrate simply as workers and that they are not interested in becoming citizens. Hence, there has been little encouragement from INS offices, particularly those in the Southwest, for Mexicans to become citizens. The actions of the INS have thus served to promote the myth that Mexicans do not come to the United States to live. The fact that the language requirement for naturalization is waived by INS for persons over the age of 50 who have resided in the United States for 20 years, for example, is one of the most well kept secrets. This piece of information is particularly relevant to the Mexican immigrant community since there is a large number of monolingual Spanish speaking Mexicans in the Untied States who would qualify for this waiver. Yet, not a single individual that we interviewed or mentioned this to was aware of such a policy.

A second issue faced by INS is the backlog of cases. Most of the INS offices located in cities with large Mexican immigrant populations (e.g., Los Angeles, San Francisco, and San Antonio) currently face a backlog of anywhere from 14 to 18 months. Undoubtedly, this backlog acts as a deterrent in some cases, particularly with individuals who may already be somewhat apprehensive about going through the process.

3. Outreach Programs

Although for many years the United States has had outreach programs to assist Mexican, Central American, South American, and other Latin immigrants to obtain legal residency, no such historical effort has been mounted in a systematic manner to assist potential citizens. While historically naturalization programs can be found in almost every city with a large Mexican immigrant population, extensive, systematic efforts have been lacking until recently. On March 15, 1984, MALDEF started an outreach assistance program in San Antonio, Texas, that has proved most successful. By the end of 1985, 577 persons had already enrolled in citizenship classes, of whom 425 (73 percent) had already applied for naturalization, although the program was planned for only 50 participants.

4. Naturalization Requirements

While there seems to be some confusion and in many cases simply a lack of information about the requirements for citizenship, two of the specific requirements pose a particular deterrence for many Mexican immigrants: language and the oath of allegiance.

The language requirement is one that, although not specifically intended to discriminate against Mexican immigrants, certainly works to keep them from becoming citizens since most of them are monolingual Spanish speakers. Obviously, immigrants from English-speaking countries have an *a priori* advantage in meeting the language requirements over immigrants from countries where English is not the native language.

The oath of allegiance also acts against naturalization for Mexican immigrants. Since the oath of allegiance also includes renouncing all allegiance to former country, it is very difficult for Mexicans to "voltiarle la espalda a México" (turn one's back on Mexico). There is a good deal of confusion among some people who believe that this literally means stepping on the Mexican flag and renouncing one's cultural heritage, as evidenced in some of the comments from respondents in our sample.

This is not to imply that Mexican immigrants are not patriotic toward the United

States. The number of non-citizen Mexican immigrants who have served in the United States military attests to the contrary. The phenomenon, rather, is a reflection of the patriotic socialization received in Mexico. As noted by Walker (1923:466):

> It would be disloyal to Mexico to adopt another *patria* (country); unfaithful, almost treacherous.

Most of the individuals we interviewed expressed this attitude. Moreover, the strength of their conviction was overwhelming.

5. Benefits and Costs of Naturalization

Although there are a number of specific rights and responsibilities that are acquired through naturalization, for Mexican immigrants they may be nominal at best and in some cases actually perceived as costs. Our research indicates that legal residents generally believed it important to become citizens but they saw citizenship as not providing specific tangible benefits that would immediately enhance their own lives. Citizenship, in other words, was not viewed as having a practical value. As noted by Ramírez (1979:10):

> It seems that most legal residents would like to become citizens, but whether citizenship is worth the trouble is another matter. In sum, the fear of institutions in combination with a lack of faith in immediate or tangible benefits from citizenship would lead to inaction—an attitude, subconscious or conscious, to leave well-enough alone.

This view is supported by data gathered from our sample of Mexicans who had become citizens. In almost every case, the impetus for becoming naturalized had been a very specific and utilitarian matter. In most cases (about 90%) the moving force was either an interest in voting or to facilitate the immigration of relatives. However, general voting practices in Mexico and the Mexican political system where one party (the PRI) has ruled since the Revolution, in the absence of an educational outreach program about the United States political system and the meaning and importance of voting, acquiring the right to vote is not enough of an attraction to cause most Mexican immigrants to naturalize.

Cultural Forces

In asking people to present their reasons for becoming and for not becoming naturalized, we were in effect asking them, among other things, to describe the cultural meanings of being "Mexican" and to contrast those with what it would mean to become an "American." To be sure, as described in the previous two sections, there were some very non-symbolic, utilitarian structural reasons for shunning naturalization, but the preponderance of the reasoning took cultural/symbolic dimensions. In short, there appear to be a number of cultural factors that contribute to the low rate of naturalization for Mexican immigrants.

1. Family and Friends

Family and friends as well as "generalized others" play important roles in influencing an immigrant's decision to naturalize. Given this immigrant group's strong cultural ties to Mexico (e.g., during our conversations the majority of informants identified themselves as being "100 percent Mexican"), it is not surprising to find that Mexican immigrants perceive and are sensitive to pressure from their family and friends toward maintaining a Mexican identity and cultural ties with "lo Mexicano" (Mexican culture). Family pressure combined with discrimination in the United States acts as a major deterrent to naturalization.

Initially our informants would indicate that they were not influenced by family and friends in their decisions regarding naturalization, stating frequently that their friends and family did not interfere in such decisions. In cases where most of the family was still in Mexico, informants would emphatically state that the family had no influence on their decision to become or not to become a citizen. Several commented that,

Allá en México mucha gente ni sabe qué diferencia hay entre ciudadanos y residentes. Ellos piensan que cuando cruza uno la frontera ya es uno ciudadano.

Many people in Mexico do not know the difference between legal residence and citizenship. They think that when one crosses the border, one is already a citizen.

Although initially we heard this type of sentiment, upon probing and further discussion we learned that the perceptions of family, friends, and a social-psychological "generalized other" indeed mattered to the individual. Those who had gone through the naturalization process were more willing to discuss the ways in which popular sentiment impacted their decisions. They had heard from other *Mexicanos,* as a means of social pressure, not to pursue citizenship, that,

. . . tiene uno que negar su bandera. Unos dicen que tiene uno que pisotear su bandera.

. . . one has to deny one's flag. Some say that one has to trample one's flag.

Some of the other comments which reflect a social pressure against naturalization and a fear of changing as a result of it are as follows (these refer to Mexicans who have become citizens):

Se sienten mucho.

They think they are big shots.

Unos hasta cambian en su manera de comportarse. Unos dicen que hasta se les olvida el español y ya no quieren volver a hablarlo.

Some even change their behavior. Some say they even forget Spanish and do not want to speak it again.

Solo los que tuvieron una vida oficial en México son los que sí se hacen más facilmente ciudadanos.

Only persons who had an official (government) position in Mexico are the ones who easily become citizens.

(In order to capture the full meaning of the last statement one needs to understand that the Mexican masses do not hold federal government officials in very high regard.)

These types of comments were even voiced by respondents who, when asked to describe specifically how their acquaintances who had become citizens had changed, were unable to identify a particular behavior or other cultural symbol that had indeed changed as a result of naturalization. It has been our experience that in most cases, the individual basically does not change, and any change that may occur is nowhere as radical as implied by the comments above.

The relationship between family and naturalization, however, has another dimension. It turns out that one of the primary incentives for a Mexican immigrant to become naturalized is for the betterment of the family. This has become particularly true in recent years, since the change in immigration laws which make it much easier for a United States citizen than for a legal resident to help immigrate his or her spouse and other relatives. Several of the persons we interviewed were cognizant of this change in policy and had either taken advantage of it or were in the process of doing so.

In addition, there are other perceived direct and indirect family benefits that result from naturalization. Some parents, for example, became naturalized before their children reached the age of 18 so that each of the children would not have to go through the process individually. Other parents became citizens because they thought that it would help their children in school, although perhaps only in a very general way, but in some cases specifically so that they would not be discriminated against. One respondent asked:

> Porqué la ciudadanía tiene que ser algo malo? Yo no la veo así, si uno lo hace por el bien se su familia.

> Why does citizenship have to be viewed as something bad? I do not see it like that, if one does it for the wellbeing of one's family.

Another individual stated:

> Fué un descanso cuando obtuve la ciudadanía, ya pude tener a mi familia bien. Yo por mi parte sigo siendo tan mexicano como antes.

> It was a relief when I acquired citizenship, I could maintain my family well. I continue to be as Mexican as before.

And still another person said:

> Para nuestros hijos hay mejores oportunidades aquí que en México.

> For our children there are better opportunities here than in Mexico.

2. Cultural/National Identity

As noted in a previous section, Mexican immigrants tend to have a very strong cultural identity that is directly tied to being "*Mexicano.*" The dominant belief is that if one becomes a United States citizen, one will become less Mexican and in the worst scenario, one will become fully Anglocized and, thus, stop being Mexican altogether.

Such a thought creates a serious conflict in the minds of Mexican immigrants.

The majority of legal residents interviewed expressed their preference for retaining legal status that entails them to work in the United Sates for long periods of time without having to relinquish Mexican citizenship. This finding is supported by the work of Baca and Bryan (1980). A frequent comment voiced by the respondents in our study was:

Nací mexicano y moriré mexicano.

I was born Mexican and I shall die Mexican.

This was obviously a very popular saying among Mexican immigrants as evidenced by the frequency with which it was heard. Such a statement reflects a cultural and national pride on the part of the individual. Mexican immigrants indeed are generally proud of their cultural and national heritage. One of our informants who was against the idea of naturalization summarized this attitude in the following commentary:

> Tomar la ciudadanía no es traiconar a México, es como negar el origen de uno, es darle la espalda a México. Tiene uno que renunciar su bandera o lo que es lo mismo. Uno jura defenderla sobre de otras. Para mi es como hacerle algo a México y eso me dolería mucho. Yo soy mexicano y me siento orgulloso de serlo.

> Becoming naturalized is not a treacherous act toward Mexico, it is like turning one's back on Mexico (abandonment and disrespect). One has to renounce one's flag or basically do the same. One swears to defend it (the United States flag) over others. For me it is like doing something to Mexico and that would hurt me very much. I am Mexican and I am proud of it.

Clinging to a rigid Mexican identity in some cases may be a means of protection and self-preservation given the degradation that many Mexicans have experienced in the United States. Persons who have wanted to participate in American society but were not permitted because of discrimination may turn to Mexico for their identity, pride and dignity. Certainly this is understandable as a social psychological mechanism that helps maintain a positive self-concept.

It is perhaps within the area of cultural/national identity that we found the most difference between our two subsamples—naturalized and non-naturalized. Naturalized citizens seemed to have resolved the issue and arrived at the conclusion that their cultural identity need not change as a result of naturalization. Several informants from this group expressed the sentiment,

> Sigo siendo el mismo. Nada más cambié una tarjeta por otra. Culturalmente me considero como mexicano y con el favor de Dios, lo seguire siendo.

> I will continue to be the same person. I only exchanged one card for another. Culturally, I consider myself Mexican, and with God's willingness, I will continue as such.

The naturalized citizens in our sample also seem to have resolved the issue of worker vs. permanent resident. One woman commented that they (she and her husband) realized that they were not going to return to Mexico to live, "solo para vacaciones" (only for vacations). She went on to describe how they had felt as neither residing in the United States nor in Mexico prior to becoming citizens.

No nos sentiamos ni aquí ni allá, asi que la ciudadanía como que nos hizo asentarnos y establizarnos finalmente aquí. De todas formas no hivamos a regresar ya a México.

We did not feel as if we were here (United States) or there (Mexico), citizenship sort of made us finally settle and establish ourselves here. In any case, we were not going to return to Mexico (to live) anymore.

3. Language

The language requirement seems to pose a particular problem for Mexican immigrants who frequently find themselves in living and working environments that do not lend themselves to the acquisition of the English language. This is especially true throughout the Southwest where large concentrations of Spanish-speakers reside, but also extends to other parts of the United States, such as Chicago, for example.

Language becomes more of a barrier to naturalization for persons who immigrate as adults (assuming, of course, that they had not learned English in Mexico) than for those who were brought by their parents as children. Several of the respondents stated that they knew of the English language requirement for naturalization, and most of these persons had assumed that their English was not good enough to pass the examination. In discussing their lack of facility with the English language, several persons stated, ''Apenas me defiendo'' (I barely get by). Age as it related to language, however, is not completely exclusionary. We found at least one older couple who was enrolled in English classes to prepare for citizenship, the husband was in his early 60s and the wife in her late 50s.

Moreover, several of the respondents complained about the lack of formal opportunities made available to Mexican immigrants to learn English. Although they were not clear on the specific details of the program, they had heard that Filipino and other Asian immigrants were given three months of English language classes before they began working. (Their information appears to be linked to the integration programs established for Vietnamese refugees.) The important point, however, is that Mexican immigrants would take advantage of such opportunities if made available.

4. Perceived Costs and Benefits

Costs and benefits are frequently based on perceptions. Few benefits were expressed by the persons we interviewed. The majority of informants who had not obtained citizenship saw almost no benefits associated with naturalization. Even the right to vote was questioned!

Esta bien, con la ciudadanía obtiene uno el derecho del voto, pero y qué? Me va Ud. a decir que con el voto van a resolverse los problemas de descriminación? Claro que no! Esos politicos que nomás andan alborotando gente, que las minorías por acá y que por allá, ahí, ahí esta, cuando se acaban las elecciones también se olvidan de uno. La descriminación no lava a resolver un pedazo de papel, la descriminación es por el color y apariencia de la gente, es por el color moreno y el acento que uno tiene.

That's fine, one acquires the right to vote through naturalization but, so what? You are going to tell me that the vote will resolve the problems of discrimination? Of course not! Those politicians that go around stirring the people, minorities here and minorities there, that's it, and when the elections are over they forget about us. A piece of paper is not going to solve discrimination. Discrimination is based on the color and appearance of people, it's based on the darker color and accent that we have.

93

Another respondent stated his sentiment regarding the vote in a much more succint and direct statement:

> Si no voté en mi pais, menos voy a votar acá. Aquí la politica es tan corrupta como allá.

> If I didn't vote in my country, I'm certainly not going to vote over here. Politics are just as corrupt here (United States) as they are over there (Mexico).

As perceived by non-naturalized legal residents, there are also no benefits to gain in employment matters from naturalization. Several respondents focused specifically on this issue.

> Con la ciudadanía no le van a aumentar su salario o le van a dar mejor trabajo. Si me fueran a pagar cinco dólares más la hora, entonces si me haría.

> They are not going to increase one's salary or give one a better job because one became a citizen. If they were going to pay me five dollars an hour more, then I would become one.

Another informant expressed this view in very cultural terms:

> Hasta verguenza me daría el hacerme ciudadano y luego para darme cuenta que nada más me contrataran como obrero.

> It would be embarrassing (shameful) to become a citizen only to learn that I would only be hired as a laborer.

In general, persons who had not become citizens did not perceive any real direct or indirect utilitarian benefits, whether it be for political, educational, or occupational purposes. And, if one does not see any benefits to citizenship, then why go through the process, particularly when there are some very specific perceived costs.

Even the persons in our sample who had become citizens could not identify specific benefits to citizenship. They spoke in general terms about voting, schooling, jobs, and other "benefits." However, they could not identify many utilitarian reasons for becoming a citizen.

> El beneficio de la ciudadanía es algo que no es inmediato sino que se ve a través del tiempo. Sí hay más oportunidades de trabajo.

> The benefit of citizenship is not something immediate, it is seen with time. There are more job opportunities.

This last statement was made more in the tone of attempting to convince the speaker himself than the listener.

One somewhat more specific benefit identified by several of the naturalized respondents was that becoming citizens gave them a sense of settling down and becoming part of a society instead of having the feeling that one was neither living in the United States nor in Mexico.

> Se siente como si uno se integrara mejor a la sociedad. Se siente uno más seguro . . . como que le da a uno mas confianza.

One feels better integrated into society. One feels more secure . . . one seems to gain more confidence.

Antes era como tener un pie aquí y el otro allá; para caminar se necesitan los dos en el mismo lugar.

Before (I became a citizen) it was like having one foot here (United States) and the other over there (Mexico); in order to walk (move forward, upward) one needs both in the same place.

Currently the most direct benefit to be gained by Mexican immigrants who naturalize is the right to help immigrate other family members in a shorter time. This policy change is relatively new and there is no assurance it will continue for a long period of time. For many Mexican immigrants, however, it is currently serving as the main impetus for becoming citizens.

On the other hand, the greatest cost of becoming a United States citizen as perceived by the persons we interviewed (those in the non-naturalized sample) is the fear of losing one's Mexican cultural/national identity. This factor, as noted in the section on structural forces, deters many potential citizens from going through the naturalization process. As discussed earlier, there is a confusion regarding what is implied by swearing oath of allegiance to the United States and renouncing Mexican citizenship. People tend to believe that they will have to stop being "Mexican," in a cultural sense, i.e., they will have to change their values, beliefs, attitudes, and all of the other symbols that make them *Mexicanos*.

Conclusions

Naturalization rates are influenced by the many factors we have identified. For Mexican immigrants the various factors can be categorized into three broad groups— background characteristics, structural conditions and sociocultural forces. All of these major forces have operated in the same direction, i.e., to produce a pattern that has resulted in the lowest naturalization rate of any immigrant group. This pattern emerged very early and in the context of a social history of labor migration in which both the participants and the host country perceived immigrants from Mexico exclusively as workers, and not as residents and potential citizens. Hence, the United States government has never developed a systematic outreach program to integrate Mexican immigrants into American society, not even on a small scale, as it has done for other immigrant groups since the late 1800s. The government's response has been to assume that because large numbers of Mexican immigrants are not filing for citizenship, they do not want to become naturalized. Yet, with other groups (e.g., Southern and Eastern Europeans in the late 1800s and Cubans and Vietnamese most recently) an attempt was made to incorporate them into American society and into the political system through citizenship.

Given our findings, clearly it is time for the federal government (and specifically the Immigration and Naturalization Service) to re-evaluate its image of the Mexican immigrant and to develop informational outreach programs to this large and growing group of disenfranchised residents. The evidence shows that although Mexican immigrants may initially resist the idea and several important sociocultural forces work against naturalization, given accurate information and assistance in preparing for the examination, many Mexican immigrants will become United States citizens. This has been demonstrated in San Antonio through the pilot program developed by the Mexican American Legal Defense and Educational Fund. Our findings predict that similar outreach programs would be equally successful in other communities where large groups of Mexican immigrants reside (i.e., almost every city throughout the Southwest, several in the Midwest, and some in other parts of the country). Note, however, that we are not promoting a mass citizenship program that forces immigrants to become citizens nor are we promoting a pressure cooker type of assimilation. We are suggesting, very simply, that immigrants be provided with accurate information on which they (each individual) can make the decision to become or not become United States citizens. Additionally, those that want to become citizens should be assisted in the process.

The non-naturalization of Mexican immigrants is a critical issue. A country that prides itself on the political voice of its citizens cannot continue to support a system in which a large group of people are disenfranchised from its sociopolitical structure. A large-scale systematic program needs to be implemented to bring Mexican immigrants into the mainstream of the American political system. Such an effort would clearly benefit the specific individuals involved, in that they would have a voice in the political system that governs them, and it would benefit the country in that it would incorporate a marginal group into its political and social democracy.

REFERENCES

Acuña, R. 1972. *Occupied America: The Chicano's Struggle Toward Liberation.* San Francisco: Canfield Press.

Anderson, J. 1978. "A Shepherd-Policeman for New Americans." *Parade.* November 5:4–6.

Baca, R. and D. Bryan. 1980. *Citizenship Aspirations and Residency Rights Preference: The Mexican Undocumented Worker in the Binational Community.* Compton, CA: Sepa-Option, Inc.

Bahr, H. M., B. A. Chadwick and J. H. Stauss. 1979. *American Ethnicity.* Lexington, MA: D. C. Heath.

Cardenas, G. and E. Flores. 1977. "Political Economy of International Labor Migration." Paper presented at the Seventh National Meeting of the Latin American Studies Association. Houston, November 2–5.

Fernández, D. 1986. "Collision of Cultures: Integration of Mexican Immigrants into Society." *The World and I* 1 (7) 651–675.

Fernández, C. and M. L. Frias. 1984. "The Causes of Naturalization and Non-naturalization for Mexican Immigrants: An Empirical Study Based on Oral Case Histories." Final report to Project Participar. San Francisco.

Fong, H. L. 1971. "Immigration and Naturalization Laws: Today's Need for Naturalization and Law Reform." *International Migration Review* 5:406–418.

García, J. A. 1981. "Political Integration of Mexican Immigrants: Explorations into the Naturalization Process." *International Migration Review* 15:4, 608–625.

Glaser, B. G. and A. L. Strauss. 1967. *The Discovery of Grounded Theory: Strategies for Qualitative Research.* Chicago: Aldine.

Grebler, L. 1966. "The Naturalization of Mexican Immigrants in the United States." *International Migration Review* 1:17–31.

Immigration and Naturalization Service. 1910. 1966–1977, Annual Reports for each of the years cited. 1978, 1980 Washington, D.C.: U.S. Government Printing Office.

Interagency Task Force on Immigration Policy. 1979. *Staff Report.* Washington, D.C.: Departments of Justice, Labor and State.

Méndez M., M. 1984. "Los Viejos Mexicanos de Los Estados Unidos." *Nuestra Voz* 2(2) 4.

Orozco, M. T. 1978. "The Non-naturalization of Mexican Immigrants." Unpublished paper available from the author at Columbia University.

Ramírez, D. M. 1979. "Legal Residents and Naturalization: A Pilot Study." San Francisco: Mexican American Legal Defense and Educational Fund.

Reisler, M. 1976. *By the Sweat of their Brow: Mexican Immigrant Labor in the United States, 1900–1940.* Westport, CN. Greenwood Press.

Vélez-I, C. G. 1979. "Ourselves Through the Eyes of an Anthropologist." Pp 37–48 in A. J. Trejo (ed.) *The Chicanos: As We See Ourselves.* Tucson, University of Arizona Press.

Walker, H. W. 1928. "Mexican Immigrants and American Citizenship." *Sociology and Social Research* 13:465–471.

Part III

HISTORY

THE LOS ANGELES POLICE DEPARTMENT AND MEXICAN WORKERS; THE CASE OF THE 1913 CHRISTMAS RIOT

Edward J. Escobar

ABSTRACT

This paper examines a little known case in 1913 in which the Los Angeles Police Department (LAPD) brutally disrupted a rally at which Mexicans protested their poor economic situation. In breaking up the rally, the LAPD killed one man and arrested over seventy others. In the legal proceedings that followed, only ten men, all of them Mexican, were found guilty of wrongdoing. The judge, however, gave the men extremely harsh sentences declaring that he did so because they were Mexicans. This incident is symptomatic of the relationship between Los Angeles Mexican Americans and the LAPD—a relationship based on the principle of using the police to maintain Mexican Americans as a source of cheap labor for Southern California business interests.

During the 1960s and 70s, Chicanos charged that American urban police were actually an army of occupation in the barrio, helping to maintain the subordinated status of Chicanos within American society. In Los Angeles, Chicano activists focused attention on instances of police brutality and claimed that this brutality was intended to intimidate Chicanos from demanding economic, political and social equality. However, with some notable exceptions,[1] most of the anti-police rhetoric of the day provided almost no hard evidence directly linking police actions to the underemployment, low wages and general poverty that afflicted many Mexicans living in the United States. Focusing on the city of Los Angeles, this paper argues that the Los Angeles Police Department (LAPD), functioning as an instrument of local business interests, worked to maintain Mexicans as a source of cheap labor. This was done by suppressing labor union activity and other forms of social protest aimed at improving the living conditions of Los Angeles Mexicans. It examines a little known case in 1913 where the Los Angeles Police Department brutally disrupted a rally at which Mexicans protested their poor economic situation.[2]

The LAPD's attitude toward labor organizations must be understood within the overall context of Los Angeles labor relations into the early decades of the twentieth century. Los Angeles, from the 1890s up until almost the end of the Great Depression, had the reputation of being a staunchly anti-union town. To a great extent, this attitude was based on the willingness of the LAPD to break strikes and engage in other anti-labor activity. At the same time this anti-labor attitude developed in Los Angeles, Mexican workers began moving into the city at an ever accelerating pace. In the city they found themselves subordinated to low paying, menial jobs. Their attempts to organize effective labor unions or otherwise challenge their status in the labor market, met with conflict from the police. The experiences of Mexican workers were similar to those of other members of the working class in Los Angeles. However, because of their high concentration at the lowest rungs of the working class, the suppression of labor union activity had a more severe impact on Mexicans than on other Los Angeles workers.

MEXICAN WORKERS IN THE LABOR MARKET

Mexicans who arrived in Los Angeles in the early part of the twentieth century found themselves relegated to working in low paying, menial jobs. Pedro Castillo, in his study of Mexicans in Los Angeles between 1890 and 1920, shows the economic subordination of Mexican workers in the early twentieth century. Table I depicts that the Mexican workforce experienced downward economic mobility between 1900 and 1920. The percentage of Mexican workers declined in all categories except that

Table 1
The Occupational Structure of Mexicans in Los Angeles, 1900–1920

OCCUPATION	1900 %	1910 %	1920 %
High White-Collar			
Professional	2.8	1.7	1.5
Proprietorial	5.0	3.0	2.0
Low White-Collar			
Sales/Clerical	6.8	6.3	6.0
High Blue-Collar			
Skilled	10.5	10.0	9.9
Low Blue-			8.1
Collar			71.5
Semiskilled	15.4	13.0	
Unskilled	57.7	64.5	
Unknown	1.8	1.5	1.0
Number in Sample	602	1,826	5,232

Source: Castillo, "Making of a Mexican Barrio," pp. 148 and 166.

category labeled "low blue-collar unskilled." Table II compares the occupational structures of Mexicans and Anglos living in Los Angeles in 1920. The disparity

Table 2
The Occupational Structure of Mexicans
and Anglo Americans in Los Angeles, 1920

Occupation	Mexicans %	Anglos %
White-Collar	9.5	47.0
Professional	1.5	3.9
Other	8.0	43.1
Blue Collar	89.5	53.0
Skilled	9.9	28.3
Semiskilled	8.1	18.7
Unskilled	71.5	6.0
Unknown	1.0	—

Source: Castillo, "Making of a Mexican Barrio," pp. 168

between the types of jobs held by Mexicans and those held by Anglos is obvious. Forty-seven percent of all Anglos worked in white collar jobs, while only 9.5 percent of the Mexican workforce held jobs in this category. More telling is the fact that 71.5 percent of all Los Angeles Mexicans held unskilled blue-collar jobs versus six percent for the Anglos.[3]

As various authors have observed, this large, permanently subordinated source of cheap labor provided the crucial element for the economic growth of Los Angeles and the entire southwestern portion of the United States.[4] However, Mexican workers and their families did not benefit from the economic development of the region. They suffered from a lack of education, poor health and the most wretched housing conditions of any group in early, twentieth century, urban America.[5]

The economic subordination of Mexican workers resulted from discriminatory employment patterns set in the nineteenth century.[6] These patterns became more firmly established and more universally applied as larger numbers of Mexicans entered the Los Angeles workforce in the early twentieth century. As previously shown in Table I, the concentration of Mexicans in the lowest levels of the occupational structure increased during the first two decades of the twentieth century.

ANTI-LABOR ATTITUDES IN LOS ANGELES

Two factors explain the Los Angeles Police Department's pro-business, anti-labor activities. First, modern organized urban police departments came into existence during the early industrial revolution for the expressed purpose of protecting the interests of the emerging capitalist class. In the early years of the republic, keeping the peace had been a relatively simple task. Most city dwellers owned property from which they earned a living and thus had an interest in the overall welfare of their community. The main peace keeping agency during these years was the watch system used to patrol cities at night. However, increasing industrialization in the mid-nineteenth century brought about important socio-economic changes. This in turn required a change in the nature of law enforcement.

The most important of these changes was the emergence of a large impoverished population which provided cheap labor for the growing factories. The people who provided this cheap labor did not have the same stake in the community as earlier urban dwellers, consequently they rebelled in response to their difficult economic condition. Local manufacturing and commercial elites viewed these riots as challenges to their authority and threats against their increasing wealth. In response, the elites successfully urged city government to organize the police department to thwart challenges to their authority.[7] Thus, the very *raison d'etre* for modern police was protecting the power and property of the bourgeoisie. In the late nineteenth and early twentieth century the police perfected their role as protectors of the capitalist class when the latter began to feel threatened by the labor movement.[8]

Another factor which explains the anti-labor activities of the LAPD is the almost fanatical antipathy of Los Angeles capitalists toward organized labor. The man most responsible for the pervasiveness of anti-labor sentiment in Southern California was General Harrison Gray Otis, owner of the *Los Angeles Times*. As a traditional conservative, Otis believed labor did not have any legitimate role in the decision making process of his business. He saw his workers as just another commodity necessary for publishing his newspaper. Otis especially disliked the closed shop, whereby employers agreed to employ only union members. If all the employees in a given enterprise were union members, Otis correctly reasoned, the employer would have to consider the union's position rather than just the welfare of the company when making business decisions. To an authoritarian like Otis, this was not only bad business but philosophically unjustified. Thus, maintaining the "open shop" became the rallying cry for Los Angeles employers from the turn of the century to the beginning of World War II.

While Otis maintained a philosophical aversion to unionism, he also fought labor activism for more practical reasons. In 1888, two years before the newspaper strike, Otis convened a group of Los Angeles businessmen to develop strategies to overcome a local but devastating depression. These businessmen concluded that only by securing a sound industrial base could economic stability be maintained. They formed the Los Angeles Chamber of Commerce with the expressed purpose of attracting more business, capital and cheap labor to the city. Los Angeles, however, had one great disadvantage in this endeavor: it had to compete with San Francisco. This northern city had a fine harbor, a rich hinterland and a forty-year head start in the accumulation of capital and industry. Its only apparent disadvantage was a relatively high wage scale. General Otis and his friends therefore came to two conclusions: 1) the only way to compete with San Francisco was to undercut the San Francisco wage scale; and 2) the only way to undercut this wage scale was to eliminate unionism in Los Angeles.[9]

These conservative Los Angeles businessmen developed complex and sophisticated strategies to maintain a low wage scale and suppress the growth of labor unions in their city. In order to flood the local labor market, they embarked on an extensive effort to attract new workers into the city. While much of the labor recruitment focused on workers within the United States, some industries which sought workers for particularly low paying or menial jobs recruited heavily in Mexico.

They also used the pages of the *Los Angeles Times* to create a popular consensus in favor of their anti-union campaign. For almost seventy years the news and editorial pages of the *Los Angeles Times* were filled with anti-labor rhetoric.[10] So harsh, confrontational and effective was the *Times'* rhetoric that in 1910 three members of the Iron Workers Union dynamited the Times Building, killing more than twenty people. Public indignation over the bombing contributed significantly to the almost complete elimination of organized labor as an economic factor in Los Angeles before the Great Depression.

Another tactic used by the capitalist class was the formation of employers' organizations such as the Merchants and Manufacturers Association, which supported businesses faced with labor disputes. This support took a variety of forms. In some cases, the employers' organizations gave monetary assistance to businesses that were being struck. In other cases, the associations provided logistical assistance, such as special guards which protected strikebreakers and helped keep businesses functioning. In still other cases the employers' associations, through the pages of the *Times*, gave Los Angeles employers advice on how to maintain the open shop.[11]

The *Times* remained a strong enemy of organized labor. Also the employers' associations gained strength through the Great Depression. However, the tremendous success of the capitalist class in Los Angeles would not have been possible without the active support of city government. City officials, usually successful businessmen themselves, regularly assisted employers by passing anti-union and anti-radical ordinances, awarding contracts to non-union companies, prosecuting pickets and generally giving support to open shop forces. The agency of city government which took the most direct role in protecting employers' interests was the Los Angeles Police Department.

The LAPD performed several important functions in helping to maintain the open shop. At the most elementary level, the police helped employers break strikes by protecting scabs and arresting pickets. Second, the police broke up public demonstrations which they deemed to be pro-labor or radical in nature and therefore potentially harmful to the open shop consensus. The police also infiltrated labor unions, radical organizations and even liberal civil rights organizations. Once having infiltrated these organizations, they obtained access to membership lists, gained prior knowledge of their activities, and even acted as *agents provocateur*. Often the LAPD acted within the letter of law in performing its pro-open shop functions. Other times, however, the police brutally and violently broke up picket lines and "subversive" demonstrations, harassed members of those organizations and generally violated the civil rights of individuals who the police saw as threats to the existing economic order.[12]

The anti-labor, anti-radical activities of the Los Angeles Police Department had a profound effect on local Mexicans. Mexican immigrants in Los Angeles worked primarily as unskilled blue-collar workers with concomitant low incomes. In order to improve their economic situation, Mexican workers regularly became involved in labor union activity. Over the years, in industries like agriculture, segments of the railway industry, the garment industry and others where Mexican workers predominated, Mexicans often formed overtly nationalistic unions which appealed to the labor union traditions of their homeland. In their attempts to improve their wages and working and living conditions, the unions regularly came into conflict with the LAPD. In suppressing Mexican union activity, the LAPD protected strikebreakers and intimidated and arrested lawful pickets. They violently disrupted otherwise peaceful Mexican labor demonstrations. Police illegally arrested men off the streets and sent them to work to break Mexican strikes. During the 1920s and 1930s, the LAPD even developed a special "Red Squad" which had the responsibility of suppressing labor unions and radical groups in Los Angeles. The Red Squad regularly violated the law by violently attacking pickets and labor supporters and, at one point, even conspiring to have the pro-labor Mexican Consul recalled.[13]

THE CHRISTMAS DAY RIOT

While many Mexicans were active in unions affiliated with the American Federation of Labor (AFL), it was the Industrial Workers of the World (IWW) who most actively and most effectively recruited Mexican workers in the Los Angeles area in the early years of this century. The IWW, founded in 1905 as an alternative to the AFL, had a well defined anarcho-syndicalist philosophy. While the AFL restricted itself to organizing workers in skilled trades, the Wobblies, as they were called, wished to organize all American workers in order to form "One Big Union." Once this union was formed, the workers would take over not only the factories, but also the machinery of government. Thus, IWW philosophy foresaw not only the end of capitalism but also the end of government as it was then defined. Furthermore, the Wobblies espoused the concept of "direct action" in order to achieve their goals. They demanded the right to defend themselves against the hostile forces of capitalism. Consequently, the IWW was the only national labor organization to make sustained efforts to organize unskilled workers like Mexicans. This was of dubious benefit to Mexicans since American capitalists and their allies in government used all means at their disposal, including violence, to destroy such a dangerous organization. Nevertheless, for many Mexicans who were familiar with and supported the anarchist philosophy of Mexican revolutionary Ricardo Flores Magón, the IWW rhetoric must have had a familiar and welcomed ring.

The Christmas Day riot of 1913 is an example of how violent police methods were used to suppress Mexican IWW activity. The riot occurred at the Plaza, a traditional gathering place in downtown Los Angeles for the local Mexican community. It occurred as a result of police breaking up a Wobbly-sponsored rally protesting unemployment in Los Angeles. The nation as a whole had been hit with a mild depression in the fall and winter of 1913. Los Angeles, however, suffered more than most cities because the intensive labor recruitment efforts of the Chamber of Commerce and the railroad industry had flooded the local labor market. The unemployment situation was particularly difficult for Mexicans. Three days before the riot, a group of 250 Mexicans gathered in front of police headquarters. According to police, "some jokers" had told them they could obtain work there. Mexican members of the IWW called the rally to protest the continuing recruitment of new workers into the city and to ask the city government to help unemployed men and women find jobs.[14]

On a rainy Christmas Day five hundred men and women, most of them Mexicans, gathered in the Plaza at 2:00 in the afternoon to hear the speakers. The rally had been in progress for an hour and a half before the police arrived. What happened next became a matter of much debate. Police Lieutenant Herman W. R. Kreige said the trouble started when he and five other officers attempted to enforce a city ordinance which forbade giving speeches in public parks without a permit. In a statement given to the *Times*, Kreige stated that when he arrived at the Plaza "a man was on the stand addressing the crowd in Spanish. I touched him on the leg and said: 'Say, mister, you're not allowed to speak in the park without a permit.' " According to Kreige, he repeated his request because the speaker ignored him. "Then," Kreige stated, "I heard someone in the crowd shout something about 'go at 'em boys' and at the same time someone struck me on the back of the head." The police drew their weapons in self-defense, Kreige maintained, but the crowd continued to throw stones at them. At one point Officer Alfred Koenigheim saw Rafael Adames point a "vicious-looking .38" gun at a fellow officer, whereupon Koenigheim shot and killed Adames.[15]

The story told by civilian witnesses differed significantly from the police version. According to these witnesses, the main speaker at the Plaza that day stood on a chair atop a table when the police arrived. Mrs. E. Tatum stated that Kreige went up to the speaker, brusquely ordered the Mexican to stop his speech and, at the same time, pulled the chair out from under him. When a Mexican bystander protested the policeman's actions, Kreige "replied by striking the [man] violently in the forehead with his club, leaving a great triangular gash from which the blood flowed freely." Although no order to disperse had been given, the crowd had started leaving the Plaza when the police first arrived. Nevertheless, according to several civilian witnesses, after the police had attacked the speaker, they proceeded to wade through the scattering crowd, hitting people with their clubs as they went. Not satisfied with moving people out of the Plaza, they began chasing people in the streets and beating them with their clubs.[16]

At first the crowd did not respond. However, according to one unidentified observer the crowd soon began pelting the police with stones. The police retaliated, this observer contended, by attempting to make arrests. Eventually, the crowd managed to isolate and attack Kreige.

> In almost less time that it takes to tell it, [the observer stated], the crowd around Kreige broke away and he emerged with the blood streaming down both sides of his face. It was before and after this scrimmage that most of the stone-throwing by the crowd and shooting by police occurred, and it was said at the time that one man was killed and carried away.[17]

Other witnesses corroborated this story but added that after the assault on Kreige, the police started firing indiscriminately into the crowd. Thus, the pro-labor paper, the Los Angeles *Record*, accused the LAPD of "cossackism" for the way the police conducted themselves at the Christmas Day disturbance.[18]

As the riot began to subside, the police became increasingly aggressive in their attempts to punish the rioters. The *Times* reported that at 8:00 in the evening police detectives began an invasion of Mexican restaurants, poolhalls and motion picture theaters and "every man who appeared disarrayed in dress, showed indication of having been through the battle or bore blood marks, cuts or fresh bruises, was jerked from his seat and thrown into the patrol wagon." In total, the police arrested seventy-three men, of which fifty-six were Mexican.[19]

Police and city officials responded to the Christmas Day disturbances by calling for further restrictions on the right of free speech. Without knowing the contents of any of the speeches given at the Plaza, Chief of Police Charles Sebastian stated:

> The time has come when this city must put a curb on the preaching of direct appeals against law and order . . . We propose to curtail these speakers who spread their appeals to the ignorant and inflame them against law and order. From this time onward we shall use every means within our power to keep these

trouble makers within strict bounds. Any further attempts to arouse their listeners against the law and the men appointed to preserve the peace will be promptly suppressed. We mean business: *liberty shall not be made license in Los Angeles* [my emphasis].[20]

Acting Mayor Frederick J. Whiffen called upon the City Council to pass a resolution "pledging Chief Sebastian its most hearty support in ridding the city of these public appeals of the malcontents desirous of stirring up the bitterest strife." Other council members wanted the police to take even harsher measures against the IWW. Councilman M. F. Betkouski stated the "troublemakers . . . should and must be firmly suppressed," and called upon the City Council "to back Chief of Police Sebastian in any efforts he may make to rid the city of this disturbing element." Finally, Councilman J. S. Conwell declared that the police should take "a stand to clear out of this city the agitators who have been doing their utmost of late to stir up trouble."[21]

Despite the exhortations of these city officials, the LAPD took no drastic actions against the Mexican Wobblies at this time. Instead, city officials sought to make examples of the people arrested during and after the riot by prosecuting them to the fullest extent of the law. In order to justify this, public opinion had to be convinced that the Wobblies, and not the police, were responsible for the riot, and, of course, the prosecution had to be successful in court. City and police officials had the firm support of the *Times* in these efforts. The Los Angeles Labor Council, the local Socialist Party and the Los Angeles *Record* generally opposed the city's position.

Almost from the very beginning, city officials and their supporters claimed that the riot had been caused by organized labor and its allies in the news media. In particular they blamed the *Record* and,to a lesser extent, the Los Angeles *Express* for the riot. Two days after the riot, an article on the front page of the *Times'* local news section stated that "in reality" the Christmas Day riot was "caused and conducted by loafers, reds, I. W. W.'s and boasted anarchists." In the same news story the *Times* claimed that "indignation against the *Record*, which is held almost directly responsible for the meeting and its dire results, was rife among the law-abiding citizenry of the city." Law enforcement officials also maintained that the IWW had actually planned to incite a riot. The police gave as evidence reports that the Wobblies had stockpiled rocks around the Plaza to use when the trouble broke out. The police also issued a statement that an unidentified Wobbly had told a "disguised detective" that the IWW had started the riot in order to get more publicity. "We've got to get into the newspapers some way,"the anarchist was reported to have said, "and if we cannot arouse them to talk about our hall meetings, then we'll have to incite news matter of some sort, no matter what the cost. The doctrine must be spread."[22]

The showcase for the city's official position in the days immediately following the riot was the investigation conducted by the Public Safety Committee of the City Council. From the beginning of this investigation, it seemed obvious that the committee would issue a report favorable to the police. On the first day of the Committee hearings, only one civilian, an arrested Mexican member of the IWW, was allowed to testify. All the other witnesses were policemen and, according to the *Record*, they all gave exactly the same story. The investigation would have ended after only one day had not the *Record* and other members of the City Council pressured the Committee Chairman, John W. Snowden, to hear more testimony from non-police witnesses. Despite the fact that all the civilian witnesses contradicted the police version of the riot, the Public Safety Committee issued a report fully exonerating the police. This report, adopted by the entire City Council, referred only to the testimony from the police witnesses and completely ignored civilian witnesses. It stated that "the police department was within its rights in enforcing the provisions of the [public speaking] ordinance." The only hint of criticism of the LAPD was that the police "might have used a little more discretion and tact in handling the situation as it existed."[23]

The *Record* and organized labor in Los Angeles came to a totally different conclusion. The *Record* reported that the civilians who testified before the City Council's Public Safety Committee clearly demonstrated that the police had caused the riot. These witnesses stated that some plain clothes policemen already had their weapons drawn before Lieutenant Kreige arrived at the Plaza; that Kreige and his men, "with drawn clubs and revolvers, knocked the crowd right and left in pushing their way to the speaker's stand;" that the police knocked the speaker off his platform; and "that the police started using their clubs before they were attacked." The *Record* thus concluded that "the testimony of unbiased and unprejudiced witnesses . . . showed up the cossack methods of the police . . . discredited the police stories of the affair and clearly indicated that the action of the police started the riot [and] that the police acted with unnecessary and unwarranted brutality."[24]

Different opinions regarding the Christmas Day riot were also voiced at meetings of organized labor in Los Angeles. At a December 27 meeting of the Central Labor Council, Socialist City Councilman Fred Wheeler declared that the railroad companies and other public utilities were at least partially responsible for the riot because they had imported hundreds of Mexican workers who were now unemployed.[25]

The *Times* reported that at a meeting the following day at the Labor Temple, "the rioters . . . were eulogized as heroes and martyrs in impassioned addresses and the policemen who courageously enforced the law . . . were hissed, sneered and called 'Cossacks, criminals, fiends' and other pet Socialist names." At the same meeting a resolution was passed condemning the "brutality of the police" and "demanding that the city council impress upon the police department that its duty is not to beat up, but to protect the public and that the police should not use violence in the discharge of their duties except in self-defense." Similar proclamations were made at other labor meetings and, for a time, a demonstration to protest unemployment and the activities of the police department was contemplated. However, the demonstration never took place because the organizers feared more police violence.[26]

The criminal prosecutions against the men arrested at the riot revolved around the same basic issue: responsibility for the violence. The first legal proceedings against the men came on December 29 when forty-four of the seventy-three men originally arrested were arraigned before the police court. All but two of the men arraigned were Mexican.[27] The *Times* reported that the "I. W. W. labor-union-Socialist gangsters" were charged with rioting for which the maximum penalty was two years in jail and a fine of $2000. At the arraignment hearing, defense attorneys argued for separate trials for each of the defendants, but the judge ruled against them and set the trial date for January 21, 1914.[28]

The trial began on time with several hundred Mexican supporters of the defendants being turned away from the courtroom. The first order of business was selecting a jury and, while chief defense attorney Job Harriman tried to choose an impartial panel, the occupations of the jurors indicated that their economic interests made them hostile to the defendants' political philosophy. Of the eleven men for whom occupations were published, three were listed as real estate agents, two as professionals, two as ranchers or farmers, two as merchants, one as a manufacturer and one as a plumber. All of the jurors were Anglo males.[29]

The basic strategy of the defense was to discredit the testimony of individual policemen and to shift blame for the riot from the defendants to the police. Thus, on the first day of testimony, Harriman won a major procedural victory when the judge ruled that police witnesses had to individually identify every man they accused of rioting rather than have the defendant stand up when his name was called. Harriman scored a second point when he forced Sergeant W. L. Hagenbaugh to agree that the riot did not start until the police started chasing people through the streets around the Plaza. "Then why," Harriman asked the Sergeant, "did you not leave the men alone and be content with having prevented the violation of a city ordinance? Why did you not remain in the park, instead of continuing on the street?" Hagenbaugh replied that to have stayed in the park would have been to "show the yellow feather."[30]

Harriman's strategy proved to be at least partially successful when, on January 30, the prosecution moved to dismiss charges against twelve of the defendants including the two Anglos. The prosecution called for dismissals for one of two reasons: 1) no one could be found to identify defendants who had actually committed a crime or 2) the testimony against the defendants had successfully been called into question by the defense. The *Record* noted with indignation that the district attorney offered "no explanation of his reason for holding the exonerated men in jail for 36 days" and now admitted he had no evidence against them.[31]

As the trial drew toward a close, Harriman stressed more and more that the police had actually been responsible for the violence. On February 2 Harriman presented a witness who, according to the *Record*, testified that the "brutal beating[s] administered by police" to the Mexicans in the Plaza precipitated the violence and that the attack on Kreige came after the shooting of Rafael Adames. The *Record* also reported that four other witnesses gave similar testimony. A day before the case was to go to the jury, Harriman made the following statement to reporters:

> The question to be solved by the jury will be which side was guilty of rioting, the Mexicans or the police . . . That will be one of the strongest points upon which I will base my plea for my clients. It is true that the police had a technical, although certainly not a moral, right to stop the men from speaking. But I have brought out that they followed the men [into the street] and exceeded their authority and that, combined with the questionable identification that has been attempted by the prosecution, will constitute the features of our defense.

Harriman's final arguments to the jury closely followed the statement he made to the press.[32]

The soundness of Harriman's strategy was again demonstrated on the evening of February 6 when the jury returned verdicts of not guilty on fifteen of the remaining defendants, guilty on ten, all of whom were Mexican, and no decision on one. However, the celebration that probably occurred Friday night in the Mexican section of the city, must have ended quickly Saturday morning when Judge Thomas P. White imposed extremely harsh penalties on the ten convicted men. Two men were sentenced to the maximum jail term of two years, five others received one year jail terms, Pedro Coría, who had only one leg, was sentenced to nine months in jail, another man received a five month term and Leon Ygnacio, whom Judge White considered "the least guilty," was sentenced to three months in jail.[33]

The *Record* reported that in passing sentence Judge White acknowledged the severity of the sentences and "strongly condemned" the "cowards" who had attacked Lieutenant Kreige and rioted at the Plaza. Then, in a statement that is remarkable for the clarity with which it reflected the actual relationship between Mexicans and the LAPD, the judge gave his rationale for the severity of the sentences.

> I have given careful consideration to the case, [Judge White stated], and I have taken into account the nationality of the accused. If the men came from a country where they were accustomed to liberty and into a land where the iron heel of oppression was ever present, it would put a different aspect to their actions. But they came from Mexico to the United States and were allowed the full privileges that are accorded our citizens. I am going to impose sentences that will warn all such agitators that they cannot dispute men who have been vested by the people of the land with authority to enforce the laws.[34]

The irony of Judge White's statement and the whole Christmas riot incident is that Mexicans in Los Angeles did not have the full privileges accorded to United States citizens. They could not speak peaceably in a park or listen to speakers of their choice. On the other hand, they could dare to protest their economic subordination, be beaten and even shot to death by the police without the police suffering any official reprisals. They could languish in jail for over a month, as several did, awaiting trial for which the prosecution had no evidence. Finally, and perhaps most ironically, they could be given sentences harsher than the norm, as the sentencing judge himself acknowledged, precisely because they were Mexicans.

CONCLUSION

The 1913 Christmas Riot is symptomatic of the relationship between the Los Angeles Police Department and the local Mexican community in the years before World War II. The police policy was to prevent local Mexicans from taking any action that would alter their status as the main source of cheap labor for Southern California businessmen. The LAPD harassed labor leaders, broke up union meetings, violently attacked lawful pickets and took whatever action they deemed necessary to suppress expressions of working class consciousness among Los Angeles Mexicans. Thus, to the extent that the LAPD succeeded, local Mexicans became locked into the cycle of underemployment, low income and general poverty from which they suffer to this very day.

NOTES

1. For discussion and specific examples of the consequences of police activities see Rodolfo Acuña, *Occupied America: A History of Chicanos*, 2nd edition, (New York: Harper & Row, 1981); Armando Morales, *Ando Sangrando (I am Bleeding): A Study of Mexican American Police Conflict*, (La Puente, California: Perspectiva Publications, 1972); and United States Civil Rights Commission, *Mexican Americans and the Administration of Justice in the Southwest*, 1970.

2. This paper is part of broader study that analyzes relations between Mexicans and the LAPD in the twentieth century.

3. Pedro G. Castillo, "The Making of a Mexican Barrio: Los Angeles, 1890–1920," (Unpublished Ph.D. Dissertation, University of California, Santa Barbara, 1979), pp. 19–20 and 132–190.

4. For the role that Mexican labor played in the economic development of Los Angeles and the Southwest see Mario Barrera in *Race and Class in the Southwest: A Theory of Racial Inequality*, (Notre Dame, Indiana: University of Notre Dame Press, 1979); Albert Camarillo, *Chicanos in a Changing Society: From Mexican Pueblo to American Barrios in Santa Barbara and Southern California, 1848–1930*, Cambridge: Harvard University Press, 1979); and, in another context, Mario T. García, *Desert Immigrants: The Mexicans of El Paso, 1880–1920*, (New Haven: Yale University Press, 1981).

5. The housing conditions of Los Angeles Mexicans are thoroughly described in Castillo, "The Making of a Barrio," pp. 91–97.

6. Camarillo, *Chicanos in a Changing Society*, pp. 126–141. Although it covers a different time period than this study, another excellent source on the socio-economic status of Los Angeles Mexicans in the twentieth century is Ricardo Romo's *East Los Angeles: History of a Barrio*, (Austin: University of Texas Press, 1983).

7. Analysis of the origins of American urban police departments can be found in: Roger Lane, *Policing the City: Boston 1822–1885*, (New York: Atheneum, 1975); James Richardson, *The New York Police: Colonial Times to 1901*, (New York: Oxford University Press, 1971); and Center for Research on Criminal Justice, *The Iron Fist and the Velvet Glove: An Analysis of the U.S. Police*, Expanded and Revised Edition, (Berkeley, Center for Research on Criminal Justice, 1977), pp. 19–23.

8. The role of police in protecting the interests of the capitalist class during the time period in question is most thoroughly developed in Sidney L. Harring's *Policing a Class Society: The Experiences of American Cities, 1865–1915*, (New Brunswick, New Jersey: Rutgers University Press, 1983).

9. Carey McWilliams, *Southern California: An Island on the Land*, (Santa Barbara: Peregrine Press, 1973), pp. 274–277.

10. For example, Otis once described unionism as an "insufferable despotism . . . odious to freemen and injurious . . . to public safety." He stated that the union boycott was a "cowardly, mean, un-American, assassin-like method of establishing a petty despotism." Even the Union label did not escape Otis's ire. In 1900 he stated that the union label was "a form of black mail, levied by organized ruffianism upon invertebrate employers, weak-kneed politicians and poltroons who [do] not assert . . . their manhood or stand for their inalienable rights." Quoted in Grace Heilman Stimson, *Rise of the Labor Movement in Los Angeles*, (Berkeley, University of California Press, 1955), pp. 37, 110, and 248.

11. In 1903 the *Times* ran the following editorial: "Employers of labor should be ready to meet and vanquish those who make unreasonable and arrogant demands upon them. To be forewarned is to be forearmed. Employers of labor in Los Angeles, having thus been forewarned, should prepare for possible disturbances by quietly arranging with skilled working men in various parts of the country, who they may, if necessary, summon at a moment's notice by telegraph, to take the place of their present employees, in case the latter should be persuaded to walk out and leave their work. The latter might then be

notified to go about their business, and never to darken the doors of the establishment again. At the same time a watch should be kept over the weak and faithless, and all interlopers. Those who are found to be acting the part of the traitor and fomenting disturbances, should be weeded out, and replaced by men who believe in respecting the interests of their employers, as well as their own." Quoted in *Ibid.*, p. 259.

12. For a thorough treatment of the labor movement in Los Angeles see Grace Heilman Stimson, *Rise of the Labor Movement in Los Angeles*, (Berkeley: University of California Press, 1955) and Louis B. Perry and Richard B. Perry, *A History of the Los Angeles Labor Movement, 1911–1941*, (Berkeley: University of California Press, 1963). For a discussion of the LAPD's role in enforcing anti-labor and anti-radical policies see Joseph Gerald Woods, "The Progressives and the Police: Urban Reform and the Professionalization of the Los Angeles Police," (Unpublished Ph.D. dissertation, University of California, Los Angeles, 1973).

13. The best comprehensive source on Mexican labor activity in the United States is Acuña, *Occupied America*. For specific information on the police department's response to Mexican union activity in Los Angeles see Edward J. Escobar's "Chicano Protest and the Law: Law Enforcement Response to Chicano Activism, 1850–1936," (Unpublished Ph.D. Dissertation, University of California, Riverside, 1983).

14. Los Angeles *Record* (hereafter *Record*), December 22–24, 1913. It is also interesting to note that the Police Commission, perhaps because of the unemployment situation, in early December had authorized the appointment of an additional twenty-five patrolmen. Los Angeles Board of Police Commissioners, *Minutes*, December 1, 1913.

15. Los Angeles *Times* (hereafter *Times*), December 27, 1913. Also see *Record* December 26, 1913.

16. *Record, Ibid.*

17. *Ibid. Times*, December 26, 1913. It was rumored that several other people were killed by the police. However, only one body was ever found.

18. *Record*, December 27, 1913.

19. *Times*, December 26, 1913.

20. *Ibid.*

21. *Ibid.*

22. *Times*, December 27, 1913.

23. *Record*, December 26, 27, 29, 30, 1913 and January 3, 1914. Also see *Times*, December 27 and 30, 1913 and January 3, 1914. The Committee report was technically correct. The Plaza itself was a free speech zone and not subject to the public speaking ordinance. However, the speaker had placed his make-shift platform on the firmer cement sidewalk that surrounded the Plaza but which was outside the free speech zone.

24. *Record*, December 30, 1913.

25. *Record*, December 27 and 29, 1913.

26. *Times*, December 29, 1913. The *Times*, in reporting Wheeler's assertion, suggested that "the horde of Spanish-Indian half breeds" could be sent to the border area and eventually back to Mexico.

27. *Record*, December 27 and 30, 1913.

28. *Times*, December 28 and 30, 1913.

29. *Record*, January 21 and 22, 1914.

30. *Record*, January 23, 1914.

31. *Record*, January 23, 1914. *Record*, January 30, 1914. An example of the tactics used by the defense came during the cross examination of the last prosecution witness, Patrolman E. E. Brown. According to the *Record*, Brown had been saved until the end of the trial because he was the prosecution's "trump card," the kind of man who "knew exactly what he had seen and was not the character of a man to be bulldozed from his testimony." During direct testimony Brown pointed out twelve men who he stated had been throwing rocks during the riot. However, under questioning by Harriman, Brown was unable to give the order in which he saw the men committing the alleged crime or other important details of the incident.

32. *Record*, February 2, 6 and 9, 1914.
33. *Record*, February 7, 1914.
34. *Ibid*. An incident which occurred three weeks after the sentencing is of some interest. On February 25 the *Record* revealed that the convicted men had been taken to a work camp run by the County Sheriff's Department and tortured when they refused to work. According to the *Record*'s story, which was not denied by the Sheriff's office, the men's ankles were tied by wire to a Sycamore tree and their handcuffed wrists were draped back around the tree and secured by a rope. The longer the men refused to work, the higher their arms were slung over the branch. The length of time the men stayed in this position ranged from six hours to three and a half days, depending on when they agreed to join the work gang. According to Judge White, who had presided over trial and now ordered the torture stopped, the men "were standing squarely on their legal rights when they refused to work" because their case was then on appeal.

THE REDISCOVERY OF THE "FORGOTTEN PEOPLE"

Rubén Martinez

ABSTRACT

This paper assesses the socio-economic situation of *taoseños* in the light of the passage of nearly one-half a century since the publication of George I. Sanchez' study, *The Forgotten People*, in 1940. Emphasis is placed on demographic and labor market changes which occurred during this period.

Nearly five decades ago, George Isidoro Sanchez undertook the first major study of the economic, social, and political conditions of Chicanos in New Mexico (*manitos*) in general, and Taos County in particular. The results of the study were published in 1940, appearing in the widely acclaimed book, *The Forgotten People*, where Sanchez presented the problems faced by *taoseños* as typical of those faced by *manitos* in general. The problems identified by Sanchez are still evident today, and it is the purpose of this paper to assess the current situation of *taoseños*.

According to Sanchez, the general problem of the *manitos* "is one of cultural contacts and conflict—one wherein traditional cultural and geographic isolation accentuate the normal problems presented by incorporation and aggravate the deficiencies of an underdeveloped economy and of a frontier social structure" (1940:38). From this perspective the normal problems that accompany incorporation are *conflict* and *accommodation*. Sanchez argues that these problems are aggravated by the cultural and geographic isolation of the *manitos*. Referring to the *manito*, Sanchez states:

> Living in isolation, he is not only removed from the normal social contacts which would tend to improve his condition, but he is highly inaccessible, physically and culturally, to the public agencies of incorporation (1940:38).[1]

But, Sanchez is also quick to note that American society is also part of the problem:

> . . . [T]he generally inferior status held by the native New Mexican today is, in large measure, a result of the failure of the United States to recognize the special character of the social responsibility it assumed when it brought these people forcibly into the American society (1940:40).

The usual problem of adjustment that accompanies cultural contacts and conflict has in the case of *manitos* been compounded by their own weaknesses and by a neglectful host society.

The solution of the problem, according to Sanchez, lay in the United States government recognizing its social responsibility and taking measures which "will fit the New Mexican to live successfully in his present environment" (1940:97).[2] Integration, then, is presented as the solution to the problems facing the *manitos*. According to Sanchez, integration could be achieved through a systematic effort by the United States government to "socially rehabilitate" the *manitos*, equipping them with the skills to participate effectively in a modern capitalist social formation. But, it is the very nature of this modern capitalist social formation that Sanchez did not fully understand.

Implicit in Sanchez' argument is the relative openness of American society. That is, that there exist opportunities for *manitos* to move upwardly in society. Sanchez believed that if the *manito* were to rid himself of his traditional culture and learn capitalist values and skills, he would be able to compete in this society. Sanchez, however, underestimated the intensity and pervasiveness of racism in this country. Although he recognized that castes were becoming evident in Taos during the late thirties, he did not perceive the strong resistance on the part of whites to social changes guided by ideals of racial equality. The inflexibility of the principle of "white supremacy" has become quite evident in the four decades following Sanchez' study. Today, this inflexibility takes the form of the continuing "white backlash" to the Civil Rights Movement of the 1960s.

Sanchez also exaggerated the "backwardness" of the *manitos*. While it is true that modernity had not shown much of its face in northern New Mexico during the first half of this century, the people of the northern villages did not live in the cultural vacuum that so many writers in the forties believed, unless, of course, one wishes to interpret the *taoseño* lifestyle through the lens of American ethnocentrism.

Decades before the arrival of the first Anglos, Taos had become one of the major trading centers in the region (Ortiz, 1980). *Españoles*, Utes, Apaches, and Comanches traded with the Taos Indians and each other throughout the second half of the 18th Century. By the time the first Anglos arrived just after the turn of the century, Taos had a "cosmopolitan" flavor which reflected the varied influence of the many ethnic groups in the region (Bodine, 1968).

Anglos, too, became a part of this "cosmopolitan" town in the early part of the nineteenth century. Arriving in very small numbers, Anglo traders and trappers enjoyed the hospitality of the locals. Indeed, with Taos located at the southern gateway to the Rocky Mountains, the Anglos frequented the town not only to trade and obtain supplies, but to enjoy a "season in civilization." A few of them married into prominent *taoseño* families and settled in the Taos Valley.

Years later, after the Americans had militarily occupied the northern half of Mexico, such famous men (or infamous, depending on one's perspective) as Christopher Carson and Charles Bent did not fare well there. However, it is somewhat significant that the first Anglo governor of the Territory resided in Taos.

Near the turn of the century, Anglo artists began to take up residence in Taos, drawn there by the mystique of the Pueblo (Reeve, 1982). Others, less scrupulous, also began to take an interest in Taos. One of these was Arthur Rochford Manby, a well-to-do Englishman who acquired several tracts of land in Taos, many through payment of delinquent taxes. Manby's notoriety, however, stems from the devious tactics he employed to obtain the Antonio Martinez Land Grant, and his instrumental role in the founding of a secret society that collected money for himself from the locals (Waters, 1973).

Other Anglos also moved into the region over time but, to this day, they have remained a numeric minority in the region. Still, it is difficult to accept the apparently widespread view that the *taoseños* have been "culturally backward and isolated." For many years there has been a steady stream of Anglo visitors to the area. This is only significant, however, if one submits to the assumption that people who are not in regular contact with whites and their way of life are isolated and backward. This assumption was quite prevalent at the time of Sanchez' study. In addition, some children of well-to-do families were educated out of the area, especially in Bernalillo and Trinidad.[3] A few went to the major universities in the country, including Yale and Harvard.[4] Finally, men, and sometimes families, joined the migrant labor streams shortly after the turn of the century in search of seasonal employment, travelling throughout the West, the Midwest, and even the South, then returning to their mountain villages when the work was done. One can hardly call this isolation, especially since *taoseños* and other Chicanos from the upper Rio Grande area served as a pool of cheap labor for various Anglo industries.

There was and has been continuous contact between *taoseños* and the rest of society at least since the middle of the Nineteenth Century. In the context of the relationships that evolved between Chicanos and *Americanos* northern New Mexico has served as a refuge from the hostile and exploitative environment that has surrounded these people. In Taos, workers could enjoy the comforts and security provided by their kin and their own culture. They may have returned to lifestyles that have been perceived as "primitive" from the Anglo perspective, but these people enjoyed working their small plots of land in the absence of an intense racial situation. From the *taoseños'* perspective, then, this so-called isolation can be perceived as positive, for in Taos the institutionalization of American domination had not permeated the everyday lives of the people.

Today, we recognize that the United States ranks among the most racist nations in the world (Bagley, 1972; Kinloch, 1981). The accommodative situation of being "forgotten" was perhaps better than being "discovered" and invaded by hundreds of Anglos seeking to escape the problems of modern urban areas. These Anglos express a fascination for the Chicano culture and lifestyle found in northern New Mexico, but at the same time they assume an air of superiority toward Chicanos. Thus the two groups evolve slowly as distinct societies bound together by force and domination.

For numerous reasons the area consisting of northern New Mexico and southern Colorado was not a region that experienced large waves of in-migration by Anglos.[5] Of course, the people were militarily conquered, as the U.S. Military occupied the town of Taos early in 1847, a few months following a revolt by Chicanos and Indians. The socio-economic structure however was not greatly disrupted by the in-migration of huge numbers of *Americanos* as was the case in other parts of the Southwest. Chicanos constituted and continue to be the majority of the population in this region. This fact influenced the nature and frequency of contact between Chicanos and Anglos. This limited contact was accompanied by a lower degree of political, economic, and cultural domination was less as well. There was the typical landgrabbing that marked the institutionalization of a different mode of production, but even so *taoseños* and other *manitos* were proletarianized at a much slower rate than were Chicanos in other parts of the country.

Together with the effects of the Great Depression, a continual decline in landholdings among *manitos* finally brought about the collapse of the relatively self-sufficient village economy of the region (Ortiz, 1980). Coupled with high rates of natural population increase, the depressed local economy forced thousands of Chicanos to emigrate. The remaining population was forced to turn to the State for relief, thereby transforming the ruins of the village economy into a dependent regional economy marked by welfare subsidization and subsistence livestock raising and farming.

It was in the midst of the social disorganization of the thirties that Sanchez conducted the first major study of the life conditions of the *taoseños*. His study, which was sponsored by the Carnegie Corporation, clearly demonstrated the marginal and subordinate position that Chicanos in the region occupied relative to the *Americanos*. Sanchez made repeated appeals to the Federal Government to assume its responsibility of preparing the Chicano for effective participation in American society. The entire nation, however, was in the throes of the Great Depression during the early part of the thirties, and by the time that Sanchez had completed the study, the New Deal programs had brought some relief from a severely stricken economy. *Taoseños* participated in such New Deal programs as the Works Projects Administration and the Civilian Conservation Corps, but their specific needs were not programmatically addressed by the Federal Government.

The Carnegie Corporation, on the other hand, did attempt to assist the Chicanos in northern New Mexico in a more programmatic manner. In April of 1940, the Corporation committed $43,000 to be used for community and adult education in the social rehabilitation of the *manitos* in northern New Mexico. Taos County was selected as the political unit within which the project would be carried out, and the doors were opened in June, 1940, under the leadership of Dr. J. T. Reid.

Guided by the philosophy of the Sanchez study, the Taos County Project respected the perspective of the *taoseños* by placing emphasis on self-help. If anything, the project served as a catalyst for organizing the members of the various villages in the county. The project continued for approximately two years, with WWII increasingly affecting the lives of Americans including *taoseños*, and eventually bringing a halt to it. In the end, the project left no enduring achievements that can be said to have significantly altered the lives of the *taoseños*. Perhaps its most important contribution was the establishment of a health clinic that provided services to the people. A description of the project written by J. T. Reid in 1946, had, as its major contribution, a list of problems identified by the members of the different villages. Overall, the influence of this and other projects in the region was minor, with the life conditions of the *taoseños* showing little if any improvement.[7]

According to Professor Clark Knowlton (1964), efforts to improve the social and economic conditions of the region failed because they tended to adopt purely economic approaches and to disregard local social and cultural conditions, apparently on the assumption that the programs would work because they had worked in other parts of the country. Knowlton further argues that the programs failed because they were not developed on a regional basis and because local leaders were not included in the planning and implementation of them. The Taos project was an exception in this regard, but its influence, too, was minor due to it being a temporary rather than a protracted effort.[8] Whether because of a singular approach that ignored social and cultural differences or because of a lack of sustained effort, attempts to integrate the *taoseños* as effective participants in a mature capitalist social formation have failed miserably. There has been, however, no problem in integrating them as a reserve army of labor and as part of a racial system of labor.

Since the 1940's, the situation of the *taoseños* has continued to decline, with the problem becoming more acute in the past decade. A review of demographic and labor market changes in Taos County should provide us with some sense of the seriousness of the situation.[9]

Demographic Changes

Sanchez reported that in the late thirties there were seven counties in the state where Chicanos constituted more than 80 percent of the population. These counties were Taos, Rio Arriba, Mora, San Miguel, Valencia, Sandoval, and Socorro. Presently, only Mora and San Miguel have populations where Chicanos constitute more than 80 percent. The counties of Valencia, Sandoval, and Socorro have populations where Chicanos are in the minority; Taos and Rio Arriba have populations where Chicanos constitute nearly two-thirds and three-quarters, respectively. The county of Guadalupe did not have a large proportion of Chicanos in the thirties, but today they comprise nearly 83 percent of its population. The counties where Chicanos today comprise more than 65 percent of the population are Mora (86.7%), Guadalupe (82.7%), San Miguel (81.4%), Rio Arriba (74.4%), and Taos (69.1%).

Over time, the population of Taos County has changed significantly without any growth of the overall population taking place. In 1940, the population of the county was 18,528. In 1980, it was 19,456, showing an increase of only one thousand persons in a period of forty years. This small increase reflects the extensive out-migration of Chicanos, especially young adults. Throughout those four decades, however, population size has fluctuated, decreasing between 1940 and 1960, then changing direction and increasing between 1960 and 1980. Though the overall size of the population has not changed much, its composition has changed considerably.

For instance, in 1940, Chicanos comprised over 80 percent of the population; but by 1960, this proportion had decreased to 69.1 percent. During the sixties the direction changed and in 1970, Chicanos made up 86.3 percent of the county's population. Change in the composition of the population switched direction again in the seventies, however, and in 1980, Chicanos again made up approximately 69.1 percent of the population.

The erratic changes in the size and the composition of the population parallel each other during those years between 1940 and 1970, after which the pattern changed and the proportion of Chicanos began to decrease at the same time that the population seems to be increasing. These fluctuations in the population signal a dramatic change in the lives of the *taoseños* in that they represent a continual proportional decline relative to members of the dominant group, the Anglos. This shift in the composition of the population increases the frequency of contact between the members of the two groups, bringing sharply into focus the racial dimension of the situation. While the Anglos have controlled the economy of the region for decades, they have not dominated local politics nor intruded much into the everyday lives of the majority of *taoseños*. In other words, the process of *inferiorization* has evolved to a lower level here than in other regions, especially urban areas. The racial roles, while crystallized, are not well-defined, with interaction between members of the different groups occurring on a more or less equal status, with the Anglos, of course, seeking to institutionalize their dominance. As the Anglos concentrate ownership of land and exercise greater control over local commerce, qualitative changes will occur in the everyday relations between the members of the two groups.

119

Labor Market Changes

Taoseños and other Chicanos in the Upper Rio Grande Valley did not engage in wage work until around the late 1870's. Prior to that, they made their livelihood through subsistence farming and livestock raising. Money played a minor role in the distribution of goods and services, with economic exchanges occurring primarily by means of barter, or the direct exchange of goods and services without the medium of money.[10] Labor was exchanged between the villagers, and they all were expected to contribute to the building of village projects, such as dams and irrigation ditches (Knowlton, 1964).

Following incorporation by an expanding capitalist social formation, the internal development of this societal group was altered by the influence of forces external to it. After the military occupation, economic dominance was institutionalized through the imposition of a new land policy and a commercial economy. Exploitation of the natural resources of the area, especially the overgrazing of land by livestock and timber cutting by the Anglos, seriously affected the relationship between humans and resources in the area (Harper, et al, 1943). The increased concentration of land in the hands of Anglos and the continued breakup of lands through inheritance further created problems for Chicanos. With the arrival of the railroads in the 1880's, many *taoseños* entered and participated in the wage system of the enveloping social formation. The expansion of mining and lumbering in the region further incorporated Chicanos within the dynamics of capitalism.

By the turn of the century, the land and the local market no longer could meet the increased needs of the local population. Men began to leave the state in search of seasonal employment. Dependence upon wage work increased for the *taoseños*, but the "quality of life" did not improve, for they were incorporated within a wage system that was characterized by a racial division of labor, thereby restricting the range of occupational roles that Chicanos could perform.

By the time that Sanchez conducted his study, the land had either been overgrazed or placed in the control of the federal government. The railroads had been built, requiring only maintenance crews; the mining booms had ended, as had the timber cycle. Many *taoseños* had left the area permanently, and those who remained were squeezed onto small plots of land that could not possibly provide a livelihood for them. Only by receiving governmental relief could the families that stayed maintain a minimum level of subsistence. In 1937, a study of the native population in the Upper Rio Grande Area by the U.S. Department of Agriculture concluded that their situation was comparable to that of tenant and cropper families in the Old South (USDA, 1937b).

Sanchez perceived the emergence of "caste lines and barriers" in Taos in the thirties, but they were already evident by the turn of the century. An important industry that emerged in Taos following the settling of the artists at the turn of the century is that of tourism. The artist colony established in Taos around that period flourished quickly and acquired for the town a reputation both in this country and abroad, especially in Europe. The result was the emergence of a tourist industry that was to shape considerably the economy of the town and county. For some of the indigenes, the emergence of a tourist industry within the local economy meant a new opportunity for employment. The Anglo-owned businesses that were established hired the local Chicanos as service station attendants, waiters, waitresses, busboys, dishwashers, janitors, and store clerks. Anglo residents also hired them as domestics.

120

The indigenes, then, provided both the commodities that were marketed (cultures) and cheap labor.

Sanchez criticizes the Anglo artists for failing to become involved in the social and economic life of the common people and to provide leadership in the solution of their problems. He seems to forget that the artists themselves had a stake in the economic exploitation of the locals. In other words, they benefited by marketing the very misery that they perpetuated (i.e., the faces of misery painted and sold by the artists stimulated the tourist industry). They may have found the culture of *taoseños* (Chicanos and Indians) quaint, mysterious, and physically satisfying, but they seldom doubted the superiority of their own culture. They deplored the isolation of the individual in modern society, but they understood or believed that it was inevitable that modern Anglo society would sweep into the dustheap of history the culture of the *taoseños*. Nevertheless, the artists sought to preserve the culture of the region and at times acted as benefactors of the people (Reeve, 1982). Such episodes of benevolence, however, did not substantially improve the economic situation of the *taoseños*, as the major determinant of their lives was the imposition of a mature capitalist economy.

During the early part of the 1930s, few workers from northern New Mexico set out from the state in search of seasonal employment. By the second half of that decade, however, economic recovery increased the number of workers who found seasonal work outside of the area. U.S. involvement in World War II affected *taoseños* in two major ways: young men left to serve in all theaters of war, and workers left the county to obtain jobs created by wartime production. As the county did not appear to experience an increase in population following the conclusion of the war, those persons who left during the war apparently did not return to the county. At the same time, out-migration of young adults from the county continued to occur. Today, many kinship ties are maintained by *taoseños* and relatives in Colorado, Utah, California, Wyoming, etc.

Since the collapse of the village economy one of the major problems of the county and the region has been unemployment. Both the county and the region have had the highest unemployment rates in the state. The data available are haphazardly collected but by using them one can develop a sense for the employment conditions in the county. Unemployment rates for the county were double digit throughout the decade of the fifties, hovering at about 12 percent. At the beginning of that decade approximately 40.6 percent of the employed labor force was concentrated in agriculture. By 1960, those employed in agriculture constituted only 14.6 percent of the employed labor force, which itself had decreased by 26.7 percent.

In 1960, the unemployment rate for Taos County was 10.2 percent, and that for the State was 5.5 percent. Eight years later, in 1968, the unemployment rate for the county was 10.0 percent, and that for the state was 5.1 percent.

To emphasize the exceptionally high rate of unemployment among the *taoseños*, it may be useful to compare it with that for Lea County, which is located at the southeastern corner of the state in an area which, for obvious reasons, is called "Little Texas." Lea County is a "white county," where Chicanos constituted only 4.8 percent of the population in 1960, and 27 percent in 1980. The unemployment rate for Lea County was only 2.8 percent in 1968, though its labor force was five times the size of Taos County.

By 1970, the unemployment rate for Taos County had decreased to 8.4 percent, but it remained much higher than those for the state (5.7) and Lea County (4.0). By 1976 the employment situation in Taos County worsened. The unemployment rate reached 17.0 percent, while the state (9.2) and Lea County (4.3) exhibited moderate and even minor increases. That year the unemployment statistic was provided for the Spanish-surnamed category by county. In Taos County, the unemployment rate for this category was 17.8 percent; at the state level it was 11.7; and in Lea County the rate was 9.6 percent. These rates clearly reveal that in both the poorest and the wealthiest of counties, and the state, Chicanos have a higher unemployment rate than the political units of which they are a part. This is nothing new, as one expects such to be the case with a conquered people, who are relegated to the bottom of society and forced to stay there. By 1982, the situation had changed very little, with Taos County having an unemployment rate of 16.9 percent, the state one of 9.2 percent, and Lea County one of 4.6 percent.

Presently, mining is the major industry in Taos County. While in 1960, only 52 persons were employed in mining, by 1977, there were 576 persons (10.4 percent of the employed labor force). By 1983, this figure had increased to approximately 1,000 persons. Should this industry collapse, and there are fears amongst the miners of plant shutdowns occurring, a large number of *taoseños* will be forced to leave their "homeland" to become part of the racial system of labor that characterizes the rest of society.

Conclusion

At present, the *taoseños* are experiencing a second major influx of Anglos into the region, the first one having occurred in those decades just before and after the turn of the century. This second influx consists of at least two major categories: hippies, who came in the late sixties seeking an escape from the nightmare of modern America, and businesspeople, who seek to commercialize the region by marketing the indigenous cultures and the natural beauty of the Sangre de Cristo mountains. Both of these groups are transforming the lives of the *taoseños* by buying up their lands and hiring them as unskilled and semiskilled workers.

The appeals made by Sanchez during the forties to the Federal Government were obviously to no avail. Throughout those decades following his efforts, *taoseños* have served as a source of cheap labor at the same time that they continued to experience a decline in landholdings. Rather than being assisted by the Federal Government, *taoseños* have been left to fend for themselves in the face of a hostile and alien capitalist social formation. In this context they have not fared well.

The *taoseños*, one of the oldest Chicano cultural groupings in Aztlán, are in the 1980's being transformed into a true proletarian group, joining the rest of the Chicanos as part of the American working class. The process of proletarianization is occurring throughout the region, and the last Chicano land stronghold is rapidly eroding, giving way to the forces of a capitalist social formation that is finally intensely transforming the regional economies of its hinterland. When the process is complete, or rather should it come to pass, the Chicanos as a racial minority in this country will become a fully proletarianized group. Their ties to the land, which are so central to their culture and world-view, will have been torn asunder.

FOOTNOTES

1. This emphasis on cultural conflict and isolation was echoed by Johansen (1942) and Burma (1949), and tended to characterize many studies of that period.
2. Such a perspective was essentially the same as that of E. Franklin Frazier, a student of Robert E. Park. Frazier argued that the only hope for Blacks in this country was integration, even though isolation had seriously impaired their ability to compete effectively with Anglos.
3. The education of *manitos* in northern New Mexico is a neglected chapter in their history.
4. One must remember that some wealthy *manito* families welcomed the *Americanos* with open arms.
5. Such reasons included the imperative of developing the coastal areas for military defense and expansion of trade. In addition, there were the many discoveries of gold, silver, and other ores in other parts of the Southwest that attracted the immigrants.
6. The concerns of the members of the village of Arroyo Seco, for example, were reported by Mr. Toribio Martinez, this author's grandfather, as follows:

   . . . (1) to protest the sale of the Antonio Martinez Grant to the Indians; (2) want reservoirs; (3) need better irrigation system; (4) want a hot lunch project [at the school]; (5) want a community library; (6) want a community center; and (7) want an investigation of water rights (Reid, 1946:30).

7. The study of El Cerrito, a *pueblito* located some thirty miles southwest of Las Vegas, New Mexico, done by Olen E. Leonard and Charles P. Loomis in 1939 and 1940, was made partly to assist in the planning of rehabilitation projects, such as El Pueblo Experiment (Loomis and Grisham, 1943). Today, El Cerrito is experiencing the takeover by Anglos.
8. One could argue that this project simply was not wide enough in scope to deal with the problems of a conquered people.
9. The statistical information provided in the sections that follow were taken from a variety of sources, all of which are listed in the bibliography.
10. There are several works that discuss the nature of the economy in northern New Mexico during the 19th Century. Perhaps the most general is that by Ortiz (1980).

BIBLIOGRAPHY

Bagley, Christopher. 1972. "Racialism and Pluralism: A Dimensional Analysis of Forty-eight Countries." *Race*, 13(3):347–354.
Bodine, John J. 1968. "A Tri-Ethnic Trap: The Spanish Americans in Taos." Proceedings of the American Ethnological Society. pp. 145–153.
Bureau of Business Research, University of New Mexico. 1984. *New Mexico Statistical Abstract. Albuquerque, NM; University of New Mexico. 1980. New Mexico Statistical Abstract. 1979–80 Edition.* Albuquerque, NM: University of New Mexico. 1970. *New Mexico Statistical Abstract.* Vol. 1. Albuquerque, NM: University of New Mexico.
Burma, John H. 1949. "The Present Status of the Spanish-American of New Mexico." *Social Forces* 28(2):133–138.
Burma, J. H. and D. E. Williams. 1960. An Economic, Social and Educational Survey of Rio Arriba and Taos Counties. El Rito, NM: Northern New Mexico College.
Harper, Allan G., Andrew R. Cordova, and Oberg Kalervo. 1943. *Man and Resources in the Middle Rio Grande Valley.* Albuquerque, NM: University of New Mexico.

Johansen, Sigurd. 1942. "The Social Organization of Spanish-American Villages." *Southwestern Social Science Quarterly*. 23(2):149–159.

Kinloch, Graham C. 1981. "Comparative Race and Ethnic Relations." *International Journal of Comparative Sociology*. 22(3–4):257–271.

Knowlton, Clark S. 1964. "One Approach to the Economic and Social Problems of Northern New Mexico." *New Mexico Business*, 17 (Sep):3, 15–22.

Loomis, Charles and Glen Grisham. 1943. "The New Mexican Experiment in Village Rehabilitation." *Applied Anthropology*, 2(3):12–37.

Ortiz, Roxanne Dunbar. 1980. *Roots of Resistance: Land Tenure in New Mexico, 1680–1980*. Los Angeles: Chicano Studies Research Center and American Indian Studies Center, UCLA.

Reeve, Kay Aiken. 1982. *Santa Fe and Taos, 1898–1942: An American Cultural Center*. El Paso, TX: Texas Western Press.

Reid, J. T. 1946. *It Happened in Taos*. Albuquerque, NM: University of New Mexico.

Sanchez, George I. 1940. *Forgotten People*. Albuquerque, NM: University of New Mexico.

Taos County Planning Commission. 1963. *Taos County, New Mexico: Economic Base and Population Studies*. Santa Fe, NM: Franke and Cornell, Inc.

U.S. Department of Agriculture, Soil Conservation Service, Southwest Region. 1937a. Village Livelihood in the Upper Rio Grande Area. Regional Bulletin No. 44, Conservation Economics Series No. 17, July. Albuquerque, NM. 1937b. Village Dependence on Migratory Labor in the Upper Rio Grande Area. Regional Bulletin No. 47, Conservation Economics Series No. 20, July. Albuquerque, NM.

U.S. Department of Commerce, Bureau of the Census. 1983. *1980 Census of the Population. Vol. 1 Characteristics of the Population. Chapter C: General Social and Economic Characteristics. Part 33: New Mexico*. PC 80-1-C33.

Waters, Frank. 1973. *To Possess the Land: A Biography of Arthur Rochford Manby*. Chicago: Swallow Press.

Williams, J. L. and P. E. McAllister (editors). 1979. *New Mexico in Maps*. Albuquerque: Technology Application Center, University of New Mexico.

LA VISIÓN DE LA FRONTERA
A TRAVÉS DEL CINE MEXICANO

Norma Iglesias

ABSTRACT

El presente trabajo es un análisis de cómo el cine mexicano, de carácter commercial, ha tratedo el tema de la frontera norte de México. Se parte del supuesto de que el cine ha jugado un papel importante en la mitificación y estereotipación de la frontera. Se analiza la producción cinematográfica desde 1938 hasta 1984 y se distinguen y describen las principales características de los 3 períodos delimitados—para facilitar el análisis. El primero comprende la producción de 1938 a 1969, el segundo de 1970 a 1978, y el último de 1979 a 1984.

Introducción

En la actualidad el cine es uno de los medios de communicación más efectivos que tiende cada vez más "a convertirse en instrumento de dominación sociopolíticas de los poderes económicos".[1] El hombre no puede sustraerse de su influencia puesto que, como dice Francisco Gomezjara, el cine se ha instrumentado en el sistema social existente para adaptarlo, convencerlo, evadirlo, tranquilizarlo o divertirlo. El cine como espectáculo está "en todas partes poniendo puntos de vista y presentando maneras de ser; el cine está constantemente sugiriendo e inventando, [aun en aquel quo no asiste al cine o al que lo hace rara vez]. Está referido al hombre y el hombre no puede ignorarlo ni dejar de sentir sus efectos".[2] El cine es en México el espectáculo público más importante. La información visual que produce, como dice Cohen-Seat y Fougeyrollas, se impone a los individuos con una fuerza que jamás poseyeron las formas de expresión del pasado. Los modelos dinámicos de esa información visual, sus patrones, tienen una potencia estructurada de un tipo nuevo, que actúa por vía insólita sobre la personalidad de quienes la reciben: su existencia social y su conducta hacia el medio se modifican radicalmente.[3]

En esta línea de pensamiento, el presente trabajo pretende ser una reflexión sobre el papel que ha jugado el cine, como integrante de la industria cultural, en la definición, caracterización y mitificación de la frontera. Se hará referencia únicamente al cine mexicano de carácter industrial, esto es, commercial y oficial, sin considerar las producciones independientes, los documentales y producciones extranjeras en general. Se abarcará un período que comprende de 1930 a 1984. La información que aquí se presenta es parte de los hallazgos obtenidos en el proyecto "La visión de la frontera a través del cine mexicano" que desde octubre de 1983 hasta la fecha la que suscribe realiza.

El cine fronterizo como género

Desde 1936, fecha en la que aparece la primera película sonora sobre la frontera, el cine mexicano ha mostrado una variedad de imágenes de ésta. Por momentos fue el lugar fantástico y violento, lleno de apaches, mineros, mujeres fuertes y sensuales de cantina y *saloon*, pistoleros temerarios y ladrones que huían de la justicia. En ocasiones ha sido el lugar de la perdición y el vicio, el lugar, casi mitológico, del placer: sexo, drogas e ilegalidad. No ha faltado también su imagen de calvario para aquéllos que con la esperanza de cruzar al otro lado son explotados, humillados y maltratados. Por aquí han pasado grandes héroes del corrido como Emilio Varela, Camelia la texana y Joaquín Murrieta. Estas tierras fronterizas han sentido las penalidades de los chicanos y mexicanos que viviendo en Estados Unidos se encuentran desarraigados y exluídos de la vida de ese país. La frontera también ha sido considerada el gran prostíbulo y el camino y destino previsto del narcotráfico. Ha sido el lugar turístico del folklore de "olé," galanes mujeriegos, mariachi y madrileñas cantando el jarabe tapatío, así como la tierra de lo que muchos han considerado agringados o pochos que para desgracia de México se han asimilado al *american way of life* convirtiéndose en probables traidores a la patria. La frontera ha sido asociada con la crisis de identidad, con la búsqueda de lo mexicano, con el conflicto y el sentimiento de sentirse amenazado de perder lo suyo. Estas imágenes han jugado un papel fundamental en la creación de mitos y estereotipos sobre la frontera; han creado todo un estilo fronterizo cinematográfico que desvirtúa la realidad.

El número de películas, las características y la importancia del impacto de las realizadas sobre la frontera norte de México, nos obliga a definirlas como un género cinematográfico: el género fronterizo. La característica central de este género radica en las peculiaridades del personaje, más que de una delimitación geográfica. El personaje de este género tradicionalmente se siente amenazado de perder "lo mexicano," por alejarse de sus raíces. En la trama de estas cintas se hace una comparación de diferentes culturas y la dificultad por asimilarse a otra que no es la propia. Existe una barrera físca y psicológica entre las dos culturas, que en la mayoría de los casos se concretiza en la línea fronteriza. Aun cuando la delimitación geográfica no es la característica central, la mayoría de las películas fronterizas se desarrollan precisamente en las ciudades de la frontera, tanto en México como en Estados Unidos. Es conveniente aclarar que en general, el cine fronterizo no ha sido un producto hecho en la frontera ni por fronterizos. La industria cinematográfica ha corrido la misma suerte que otro tipo de industrias, ha estado centralizada desde sus inicios. Por lo tanto, hablar del género cinematográfico fronterizo es hablar de un cine *para* el fronterizo y no *de el* fronterizo. También resulta conveniente señalar que dentro del género fronterizo se da otra división genérica, esto es, existen westerns, comedias rancheras, melodramas, aventuras y thrillers, entre otros.

Al hacer una revisión detallada de la producción cinematográficia mexicana sobre la frontera norte, encontramos que hasta noviembre de 1984 se habían realizado, por lo menos, 172 largometrajes sobre el tema.[4] Dentro de la producción de este género podemos delimitar tres grandes etapas. La Primera comprende de 1938 a 1969, la segunda etapa va de 1970 a 1978 y la última de 1979 a 1984.

Temática del cine fronterizo: La migración a Estados Unidos

Los primeros 20 años del primer periódo de la producción cinematrográfica sobre la frontera se caracterizaron, a diferencia de los siguientes, por la variedad de temas. En estos años encontramos principalmente películas sobre migración, el hampa y vaqueros, desarrollados respectivamente en melodramas, melodramas cabaretiles y westerns. Con respecto a la migración las primeras cintas que se filmaron fueron: *La China Hilaria* (1938) de Roberto Curwood y *Adiós mi chaparrita* (1939; antes *Los refugiados* o *Los repatriados*) de René Cardona. Ambos melodramas rancheros se centraban en las penalidades que pasaban las familias de los migrantes al quedar abandonadas. Se presentaba al migrante com un buscador de aventuras que sin remedio se "apochaba" en aquellas tierras: Salían sombrerudos y regresaban enchamarrados.

La burla a su cuestionable mexicanidad como pocho era el hilo conductor de la trama. Aun cuando toda la década de los 30 fue una época crítica e importante en los anales de la migración de mexicanos hacia Estados Unidos (por el elevado número de deportados, por el procedimiento de "repatriación voluntaria" y por la conocida participación de los cónsules mexicanos en la política fronteriza), el cine mexicano desaprovechó este contexto, por demás importante y rentable, empezando la tradición de un cine desinformado, no comprometido, ligero y ajeno a la problemática a la que se refiere. Otra de las películas sobre migración en esos años fueron: *Pito Pérez se va de bracero* antes denominada *El Inmigrante* (1947) de Adolfo Patiño Gómez, y *El Fronterizo* (1952) de Miguel M. Delgado. Ambas se centraban en la burla de los gringos, en la broma del *american way of life* y en la crítica a los pochos.

El único intento cinematográfico más o menos serio de este período sobre la migración fue el de Galindo en su película *Espalda mojada* (1953). Esta película fue calificada en su época como "una crítica honrada, realista y digna de elogios". Fue la primera cinta que en lugar de cuestionar la mexicanidad del migrante lo convertía en héroe. Su honradez y buenos sentimientos lo hacían salir adelante, además de acabar simbólicamente con todos los explotadores norteamericanos apagando la sed de venganza de miles de deportados. De esta manera se podían distinguir dos líneas opuestas en la caracterización del migrante; o bien era un ser despreciable y cuestionable por su falta de patriotismo al migrar, así como por sus costumbres agringadas, o bien se maneajaba como un héroe que al fin y al cabo burlaba a los gringos.

Para los años 60, las películas sobre migración no querían dedicarse únicamente a los problemas de los familiares de los que se quedaban, ni de las consecuencias del regreso del migrante. Parecía más rentable desarrollar fantasías a partir de las aventuras de estos hombres en Estados Unidos. El caso más ilustrativo de esta corriente fue la película *El bracero del año* (1963) de Rafael Baledón. García Riera afirma:

> Con un nombre de Natalio Reyes Colas, que venía a ser una "traducción" del de "Nat King Cole", cantante y actor norteamericano, "piporro" ilustraba en esta comedia las fantasías más desorbitadas que podían oponerse a la dura realidad del

bracero mexicano en Estados Unidos. Si la falta de papeles lo condenaba, como a tantos de sus iguales, a la pérdida de la identidad, la ayuda de un paisano, Antonio Aguilar, y su buen comportamiento . . . [como trabajador, lo restituían ganándose] la fama; el hombre convertido en el Bracero del año, recibía desde un coche descubierto, muy al modo norteamericano, el homenaje de la gente que agitaban banderas de México y Estados Unidos; se imganiba un David que enfrentaba a un gigantesco *sheriff* rubio cuya en Hollywood a la filmación de un número musical espectacular, con *girls* en línea; conquistaba a una "estrella" gringa (Kitty de Hoyos) que quedaba prendada de él; lo vestían de *latin lover* con sombrero de bolitas (música de guitarra flamenta), etc. y sin embargo, la película resolvía al final que era mejor vivir en México; "La tierra es igual aquí que alla, ¿por qué no trabajar aquí"? Así las fantasías irrealistas pretendían ser compensadas a final por la hipocresía.[5]

Ni las películas sobre migración del primer período, ni las de los dos períodos restantes reflejaron realísticamente la problemáticia de los migrantes. Casi todas las películas del género han alejado al espectador de la problemática social, que se desprende del fenómeno de la migración a Estados Unidos. Lo típico fue que se reforzara la creencia de que los problemas sociales son una cuestión derivada del comprotamiento individual, o en el peor de los casos, resultado del destino o de la mala suerte. La migración de mexicanos hacia Estados Unidos, siendo fundamental para entender la dinámica fronteriza del norte de México, ha sido pocas veces mostrada en las películas como un fenómeno complejo. Se ha visto solamente como un acto individual, como el resultado de la probreza de un mexicano del interior del país, como la decisión absurda de un aventurero en busca de dólares. Estas cintas refuerzan una ideología, como ha señalado Jorge Bustamante, que presenta a la migración como un problema que padece Estados Unidos por culpa de factores esternos que le son totalmente ajenos y que require de un remedio de fuerza, plenamente justificada porque se dirigen contra el mal. Las películas mexicanas commerciales sobre la migración le han hecho el juego a esa visión ideológica, proyectando la imagen de los migrantes como sinónimo del mal que afecta al país vecino. La mayoría han reafirmado el carácter criminal del fenómeno, uno de los muchos detalles que lo delatan es la palabra "ilegal" que tiene un profundo contenido ideológico puesto que reafirma precisamente ese carácter criminal de que hablamos.

Frontera norte: lugar de perdición

Por su parte, otro de los géneros importantes de este período fue el melodrama cabaretil (14 cintas). En estas cintas se presenta a la frontera como el lugar indicado para la mafia y la prostitución. Ciudad Juárez fue la ciudad más popular en estas cintas turbulentas llenas de explotadores de mujeres, cabareteras, bailarinas, traficantes y detectives, acompañados de violencia, abusos, asaltos y toda una serie de actividades ilícitas que caracterizan al melodrama cabaretil, para terminar, cumo buen churro mexicano, con olvidarlo todo y ser felices. Uno de estos casos es *Cruel destino* o *Allá en la frontera* (1943) y *Los misterios del hampa* (1944) de Juan Orol, *La herencia de la llorona* (1946) de Mauricio Magdaleno, *Pecadora* (1947) de José Diaz Morales y *Frontera Norte* (1953) de Vicente Orona.

No es de admirar la asociación que el cine mexicano hizo entre la frontera, en especial Ciudad Juárez, y la perdición y el vicio. No es que esto no existeria. El recientemente redescubierto escritor chicano Daniel Venegas escribió una novela en 1928 titulada, *Las aventuras de Don Chipote* que versa sobre las peripecias de los migrantes mexicanos de la época. En esa novela comenta como Ciudad Juárez era "uno de los lugares de mayor perversión . . . Es allí donde los borrachos que viven en El Paso van a calmar su sed estimulade por las leyes prohibicionistas de la época. La prostitución que es tan perseguida y castigada en El Paso, ha hecho su cuartel general en Juárez. De modo que allí, si no se encuentran industrias, se hallen cantinas, casas de juego y casas públicas".[6] Sin embargo, es lamentable que esta imagen, tan real en el pasado, haya sido mantenida por el cine mexicano como una caracterización de la frontera norte que distorsiona el avance económico, social, cultural y político que esta parte del país ha tenido.

Soy mexicano, de acá de este lado

Otro de los temas importantes, tanto por el número de cintas producidas como por el impacto en la creación de estereotipos del fronterizo, fue el que se refiere al folklore, al nacionalismo y a los pochos. Películas como *Primero soy mexicano* (1950), *Acá las tortas* (1951), *Soy mexicano de acá de este lado* (1951) y *La güera Xochitl* (1966) son algunos ejemplos. Estas cintas se caracterizan por soslayer el problema de la migración presentando un nacionalismo irracional. "Llenas-como dice García Riera-de un odio a los gringos, con toda su carga de fustraciones y complejos. La figura del pocho, además de resultar ridícula era sospechosa de traición y, con todo, en el fondo envidiable".[7] En *Acá las tortas* de Juan Bustillos Oro, un matrimonio de torteros, despúes de muchos sacrificios, mandan a sus hijos a estudiar a Estados Unidos. El drama se presenta cuando los aprochados hijos regresan y se avergüenzan de sus padres, planteándose la tragedia de identidad cultural, como dice García Riera, hasta niveles gastronómicos.[8]

El último ejemplo de películas sobre pochos en este período fue precisamente la cinta *El pocho* (1969), escrita, dirigida, producida y actuada por "El Piporro." Esta película buscaba, según dice el actor, la dignificación y comprensión del pocho con sólo barnices de buen humor.[9] Sin embargo, y a pesar de las buenas intenciones, la película, como varias organizaciones chicanas lo manifestaron a la opinión pública mexicana, resultó insultante y estúpida, y contribuía a la discriminación de los chicanos. En nombre del humor que ya había caracterizado al actor en sus anteriores películas, sedesvirtuaba la problemática tanto de los chicanos como de los trabajadores migrantes.

Por otro lado, en los últimos años de esta primera etapa la comedia ranchera y sobre todo el western fueron los géneros más importantes. La década de los 60 estuvo dedicada, en cuanto to producción fronteriza se refiere, casi exclusivamente a ellos. Tan sólo entre 1955 y 1966 se realizaron, por lo menos, 29 películas de este tipo, entre las que encontramos *El terror de la frontera* (1961), *La Vieja California* (1962), *La frontera sin ley* (1964), *Los Sheriffs de la frontera* (1964), *Sangre en el Río Bravo* (1965), y las 5 películas sobre el texano de Alfredo B. Crevenna. Los westerns fronterizos no variaban mucho del resto de los westerns mexicanos; en todos ellos aparecían pistoleros, robos y pasiones amorosas con las güeras. Sin embargo en los westerns fronterizos se cuestiona de alguna manera, las diferencias culturales entre México y Estados Unidos. Algunos de ellos se desarrollan en California en el siglo XIX en el momento en que estas tierras pasan a formar parte de Estados Unidos. Otros en alguna ciudad fronteriza, real o imaginaria. Uno de esos lugares imaginarios y fantásticos fue el pueblo de "Frontera Triste" de la película *Pancho López* (1956) de René Cardona. Algunas de las comedias rancheras y de los westerns que se desarrollan en épocas más recientes aparecen vaqueros y bandoleros, pochos como Mike y Bill en la película *Alma grande* (1965). En estas películas se producían los mismos estereotipos del western norteamericano. Los mexicanos aparecían "de bigote, con sombrero y carrilleras, siempre sucios y deprivados y con botella de tequila en la mano",[10] distinguiéndose muy bien del héroe norteamericano.

Segundo período del cine fronterizo.

El período, 1970 a 1978, fue muy importante para el cine fronterizo, y en general para el cine nacional. La conocida "apertura democrática" en el sexenio de Luis Echeverría y el interés y apoyo económico que se le dio a la industria cinematográfica como solución a la crisis de esta industria se vio reflejada en el tratamiento del cine fronterizo. Como ha comentado David Maciel, el cine podía ser utilizado para reforzar el nacionalismo cultural, para reflejar las cuestiones críticas, para promover la unidad del Tercer Mundo y para dar una impresión general de la nueva dirección del estado mexicano.[11] De este modo se incorporaron a la producción cinematográfica intelecuales y nuevos artístas que habían sido limitados en sexenios pasados y que se oponían a la antigua política nacional cinematrográfica.

A partir de 1970 el género fronterizo se consolida verdaderamente como un género. En ese intento de unidad tercermundista, la frontera, ya no mayoritariamente de westerns, que al fin y al cabo eran abstractos para el público por lo lejano que aparecían en el tiempo, toma fuerza cinematográficamente con temas sobre migración y chicanos. A partir de este cambio temático se logró atraer un público más amplio, ya no concentrado en los mexicanos, sino en la población mexicana, latinoamericana y mexico-americana en Estados Unidos. La participación en la producción personas comprometidas con las temáticas tratadas, permitió que en medio de los churros mexicanos aparecieran productos serios, comprometidos y de calidad como la película *Raíces de sangre* (1976) del chicano Jesús Treviño con actores también chicanos. Sin embargo, la mayoría de los productos del cine comercial utilizaron el auge de los temas fronterizos como chicanos, migración y contrabando y traición para acrecentar sus ganancias. La producción comercial del género fronterizo aumentó notable-mente, no porque hubíera una preocupación por los problemas sociales de la fronteria, como fue el caso de algunos directores como Jesús Treviño, sino porque se descubren las posibilidades de un mercado para este tipo de películas y con ello las posibilidades de aumentar, aun más, las ganancias. Un buen ejemplo de lo anterior lo constituye la película *Soy chicano y mexicano* (1973) de Tito Navarro con los actores más populares del género fronterizo, Cornelio Reina y Ana Bertha Lepe. La cinta aprovechó el interés que había en esos años por el movimiento chicano para desarrollar un nada original melodrama lacrimógeno, en donde el migrante, en contra de los deseos de su querida novia, decide migrar an Estados Unidos. Lo especial de este film fue que Cornelio Reina, haciéndole del chilango Efrén Torres, decide migrar porque es la única manera de aprender bien el inglés: "en estos días—dice el protagonista en la película—es un requisito indispensable para conseguir trabajo". No bien cruza la frontera Efrén cuando es deportado. Vuelve a cruzar la frontera en la cajuela de un automóvil. En San Antonio se pone en contacto con sus parientes y a través de ellos consigue trabajo. Se da cuenta de cómo viven los chicanos, y un buen día, después de muchas penalidades, es deportado nuevamente. Llega a México y va en busca de su novia, que, para su desgracia, se ha casado con un hombre rico.[12] Moraleja: no te cruces la frontera porque pierdes la novia; y si quieres aprender inglés, búscate una academia cercana.

A partir de los años 70 la mayoría de las películas fronterizas se estrenan an Estados Unidos, teniendo elevadas ganancias en dólares. Esto atrajo todavía más la atención de los productores, por lo que en sólo ocho años se filmaron, por los menos, doce películas sobre migración entre las que encontramos *Deportados* (1975), *El illanto de los pobres* (1977) y *Wetback (Mojado)* 1977; nueve películas sobre chicanos como *Soy chicano y mexicano* (1973), *El chicano justiciero* (1974), *Contacto chicano* (1977), siete cintas al estilo de contrabando y traición como *La banda del charro rojo* (1976), *Mataron a Camelia la texana* (1976), *La muerte del soplón* (1977) y *Contrabando por amor* (1978), seis westerns como *Somos del otro Laredo* (*Chicanos go home*, 1975) de los polivoces.

Tercer período

El éxito del cine fronterizo y la posibilidad de abrir más mercados en Estados Unidos a través de la distribución de películas Azteca Films en Los Angeles sirvió de trampolín para la producción de lo que denominaremos el tercer y último período del cine fronterizo que abarca de 1979 a 1984. Este período se ha caracterizado por las derivaciones más aberrantes del género. En seis años de este período se han hecho, por lo menos, 43 películas, encontrándose a la delantera los melodramas sobre migración (21), en seguida las aventuras de contrabando y traición (19) y tan sólo dos melodramas sobre chicanos y un western. Dentro de las películas sobre migración tenemos los casos de *La ilegal* (1980), *Mamá solita* (1980) y *Las braceras* (1981); en las aventuras de contrabando tenemos casos como *La Mafia de la frontera* (1980) *Asalto en Tijuana* (1984) y *Lola la trailera* (1984), película ésta que el pasado agosto se estrenó en 50 salas de E. U. simultáneamente.

A manera de conclusión

La pregunta medular que nos sugiere todo lo anterior es ¿por qué, a pesar de que estas películas son temáticamente y técnicamente tan malas, se siguen produciendo aun en mayor número? Una respuesta inmediata es que existe un público creciente que asiste a las salas de cine a verlas. El género fronterizo tiene una ventaja muy importante que se aprovecha a nivel de mercado; el tema abarca un auditorio muy amplio. Habría que considerar que en México todos somos migrantes en potencia; la idea de cruzar "al otro lado" es una esperanza ya convertida en mito para un elevado porcentaje de mexicanos. Ellos constituyen el público idóneo para las películas fronterizas además de los aproximadamente cuatro millones de ciudadanos mexicanos residentes en Estados Unidos, con y sin papeles; así como los cerca de quince millones de estadounidenses de origen mexicano. Ellos forman un mercado ansioso y ávido de cine que los refleje, que los represente y los haga sentir integrados, aunque sea en los churros fílmicos, a la realidad nacional. Estas películas explotan el deseo recóndito de los mexicanos de ir a Estados Unidos, o viceversa, de regresar algun día a su querido México.

El cine fronterizo, como posiblemente la mayoría del cine nacional, indica la constante de una imagen de la frontera desde la ciudad de México. El peligro es grande cuando los estereotipos se toman como realidades sin que haya una conciencia clara de que estas imágenes se hicieron para ganar dinero. La ficción se convierte en una realidad sobre la realidad o como hubiera dicho el sociólogo norteamericano W. I. Thomas "cuando la gente cree qua las cosas son reales esas cosas se convierten en reales en sus consecuencias". La visión de la frontera a través del cine mexicano es una consecuencia de un centralismo que tiende a la imposición etnocéntrica de una definición de la realidad para consumo obligado de quienes la viven aun en contra de lo que están viviendo, abriéndose una brecha enorme entre el mundo de la vida cotidiana y el mundo de la cultura cinematográfica.

La definición de la realidad fronteriza ha dependido de la propiedad y el control sobre los medios de producción cinematográfica que no han estado en manos nunca de una población fronteriza. Esto refleja una dimensión de la desigualdad nacional en la cual hay grandes sectores de la población y regiones del país quienes han visto cancelado su derecho de expresar cinematográficamente quiénes son, cómo son y hacia dónde quieren ir. Para el caso del género fronterizo, los mediosde producción cinematográfica han estado en manos de pocas familias como los Galindo y los Aguilar entre otros.

Las distorsiones de la realidad se dan a tal grado que se convierten en obstáculos para el encuentro con la realidad, y al mismo tiempo, paradójicamente, es lo único disponible como paraje cultural para la autoidentificación como miembro de una comunidad regional. Un caso muy evidente es el hecho de que para un gran sector de la población de trabajadores migrantes en E.U. y de chicanos, el cine mexicano es el único encuentro con la "cultura mexicana"; cuestionar este producto significa para muchos de ellos, cuestionar su mexicanidad y con ello crear serios problemas de identidad cultural. El cine mexicano y sus imágenes estereotipadas se convierten en el único elemento de referencia para la identidad cultural junto con el corrido. Sin embargo, el corrido ha sido históricamente una manifestación cultural popular y el cine la ha utilizado como dato, como unpretexto o como base de legitimidad de esa falsa interpretación de la realidad. Otra de las características del género fronterizo es que los productos se hacen para el consumo inmediato, destinades a morir en un año y carentes de cualquier propósito de permanencia. Es necesario pugnar por una proyección más real y crítica de la realidad fronteriza en el cine. Es necesario, como dice Tomás Gutiérrez Alea, hacer cine más fecundo para que empuje al espectador hacia una comprensión más profunda de la realidad y consecuentemente lo ayude a vivir más activamente, que lo incite a dejar de ser un mero espectador ante la realidad.[13] Para esto debemos apelar no solo a la emoción, al sentimiento, sino también a la razón y al intelecto.

Notas

1. Francisco Javier, Gomezjara y Delia Selene de Dios, *Sociología del cine* (México, D. F.: Ed. Diana, [Colección SEP-Setentas Diana, No. 110], 1981), p. 8.
2. Pablo Humberto Posada, *Apreciación del cine* (México, D. F.: Universidad Ibero-americana-Alhambra Mexicana, 1980), p. 7.
3. G. Cohen-Seat y P. Fougeyrollas, *La influencia del cine y la televisión* (México, D. F.: Fondo de Cultura Económica, [Breviarios No. 189], 1967), pp. 13 y 14.
4. Los datos que se muestran en este trrabajo fueron obtenidos a través de una revisión cuidadosa de diferentes fuentes. La fuente informativa de la que se partió fue *Historia Documental del Cine Mexicano* de García Riera. La información de 1967 a la fecha se basó en la revisión de catálogos, listas, anuarios y archivos de companías distribuidoras y productoras cinematográficas, así como dependencias gubernamentales. Se revisaron las carteleras y las críticas periodísticas de varios diarios de nuestro país. Se explotó la memoria de algunas personalidades importantes dentro de la vida cinematográfica de México y sin embargo no hay ninguna seguridad de que la presesnte información esté completa. Seguramente han de existir más películas mexicanas sobre la frontera que por distintas causas no fueron registradas. Ha existido en México una terrible laguna de información y una gran deficiencia en la sistematización de la que existe, lo cual dificulta mucho la investigación al respecto.
5. Emilio García Riera, *Historia Documental del Cine Mexicano* (México, D. F.: Ed. Era, 1975, Vol. III), p. 110.
6. Daniel Venegas, *Las aventuras de don Chipote o cuando los pericos mamen* (México, D. F.: SEP-CEFNOMEX, 1984), p. 28.
7. Ibidem, p. 339, Vol. 4.
8. Ibidem, p. 340, Vol. 4.
9. Cineteca Nacional. "Ficha técnica y testimonios de la película El Pocho" (México, D. F.: mimeo, s/f), p. 3.
10. Jesús Treviño, "Presencia del cine chicano" en *A través de la frontera* (México, D. F.: CEESTEM-Instituto de Investigaciones Estéticas UNAM, 1983), p. 195.
11. David Maciel, "Visión of the other Mexico: Chicanos and Undocumented workers in Mexican Cinema, 1954–1982" en *Chicano Cinema* (Binghamtom, New York: Bilingual Press, 1985), p. 75.
12. Cineteca Nacional, "Sinopsis de la película 'Soy Chicano y Mexicano' " (México, D. F.: mimeo, s/f) C. 1.
13. Tomás Gutiérrez Alea, *Dialéctica del espectador* (México, D. F.: Federación Editorial Mexicana, 1983), p. 36.

CONTRIBUTORS

Juan R. Garcia, Chair

History Department
University of Arizona
Tucson, Arizona

Julia Curry Rodriguez

Chicano Studies Center
University of California-Los Angeles

Clara Lomas

Christine Marie Sierra

Political Science Department
University of New Mexico
Albuquerque, New Mexico

Sylvia S. Lizarraga

Chicano Studies Program
University of California-Berkeley
Berkeley, California

Richard Griswold del Castillo

Department of Mexican American Studies
College of Arts and Letters
San Diego State University
San Diego, California 92182

Renato Rosaldo

Department of Anthropology
Stanford University
Stanford, California

Lauro Flores

Center for Chicano Studies
University of Washington
Seattle, Washington 98195

Lawrence Benton

Department of Modern Languages
California State University, Chico
Chico, California 95929-0825

Raymond Buriel

Pomona College
The Claremont Colleges
Claremont, California

Desdemona Cardoza

Analytical Studies
California State University
Los Angeles, California 90032

Celestino Fernandez

Associate Vice President for Academic Affairs
University of Arizona
Tucson, Arizona 85721

Edward J. Escobar

Department of Minority Studies
Indiana University-Northwest
Gary, Indiana

Ruben Martinez

Department of Sociology
University of Colorado
Colorado Springs, Colorado

Norma Iglesias

El Colegio de la Frontera Norte
Tijuana, B.C.